CONTEMPORARY **needlepoint**

CONTEMPORARY
needlepoint

Caroline Robins and Christine Büttner

MITCHELL BEAZLEY

Contemporary Needlepoint

Caroline Robins and Christine Büttner
Photographs by Simon Wheeler

First published in Great Britain in 1994
by Mitchell Beazley
an imprint of Reed Consumer Books Limited
Michelin House
81 Fulham Road
London SW3 6RB
and Auckland, Melbourne, Singapore and Toronto

art editor   Peta Waddington
editor   Sophie Pearse
executive art editor   Larraine Shamwana
art director   Jacqui Small
executive editor   Judith More
production   Christine Campbell

A CIP record for this book is available from the British Library.

ISBN 1 85732 258 4

The publishers have made every effort to ensure that all instructions
given in this book are accurate and safe, but they cannot accept liability
for any resulting injury, damage or loss to either person or property whether
direct or consequential and howsoever arising.
The author and publishers will be grateful for any information which
will assist them in keeping future editions up to date.

Text typeset in Janson and Frutiger
Produced by Mandarin Offset
Printed and bound in China

contents

INTRODUCTION

My passion for needlework began in childhood. I have wonderful memories of my grandmother, mother, sister and myself all sitting together in our cosy sitting room while my mother and grandmother worked on their needlepoint. Together they completed many beautiful chair seat covers, cushions and bell pulls, most of them in traditional floral designs. However, they also produced some figurative needlepoints in intricate detail. One of these was a firescreen on which a rather dapper Scottish gentleman, wearing a pair of tartan trousers, was seated reading a newspaper! I was fascinated by their work and eager to try some myself. And just as soon as I could be trusted with a needle and canvas, I began stitching too.

At the same time I was equally captivated by other beautiful objects, especially the china ornaments in our home. I can still remember my favourites and recall their shapes, colours and designs, among them some plates that my grandmother painted herself. Her designs were influenced by the Art Nouveau movement, in particular the work of Charles Rennie Mackintosh who was living in Glasgow, her home town, when she was young.

Later, at Art College in London I had the opportunity to experiment with all kinds of influences and to express myself freely. I continued to do needlepoint alongside my illustration work until I hit upon the notion of combining the two. I wanted my pictures to develop into tangible objects – to be a craft as well as an art. I little suspected, as a young art student, what a rich

above: A hand-stitched purse inherited from my grandmother.

and rewarding activity designing needlepoint would be. It has become the basis of all my artistic endeavours and has brought surprises and fulfilment in abundance. I have also been very fortunate to work with Kaffe Fassett, through whom I met others who shared my passion for needlepoint. The people, the surroundings and Kaffe himself have left a lasting impression on me.

This project is a wonderful chance for us to share the pleasures of needlepoint with you. I am sure that once you try it you, too, will be thoroughly hooked. Discover for yourself just how exciting the craft is if you take a fresh, contemporary approach. Whether you prefer simple, quick projects or more ambitious designs, you will find something to suit you among our varied collection. Needlepoint is an extremely versatile craft and can be enjoyed on many different levels. A simple design will suit those who are looking for a relaxing, therapeutic hobby, while a more complex one will appeal to those who are looking for a challenge. For those who may wish to take the creative process further, many will find it enormously satisfying to design their own work. Needlepoint accommodates itself quite happily as part of a busy lifestyle – it can be carried with you and worked on at odd moments; but it is also a delightful way to spend a long winter evening, or a warm summer afternoon, when the light is perfect for stitching. So, I urge you to try this simple and rewarding craft, not only working some of our pieces but also experimenting with your own ideas.

Caroline Robins

INTRODUCTION

I can't remember when exactly I started sewing, but I was very young. My mother used to make clothes and toys for my sister and me and we would eagerly await the scraps, which we, in turn, would make into outfits for our dolls and teddy bears. I learned cross stitch and knitting at my primary school, and later I made felt animals. My teachers tried to instil good habits like working with tailor's tacks and oversewing raw edges, but in my case it was a lost cause. I had learned to sew for the fun of it, so although my finished projects looked fine, my working methods were unorthodox. Undaunted I have continued to take a pragmatic approach to my needlepoint. I took up needlepoint six years ago. Previously I'd been making patchwork quilts, by hand, averaging about one a year! It gave me something productive to do while commuting to London from the suburbs; but quilts get very large and cease to be portable, so I looked for something else. Needlepoint was a natural choice; the challenge of creating images on a grid appealed to me and the texture of the stitched threads was very satisfying. And, of course, there were the colours. One of my favourite stages of needlepoint is selecting the yarns or threads. I can spend literally hours trying out different combinations, just holding the various strands against each other and seeing what happens. An item that I treasure is an embroidered cushion cover that my grandmother made many years ago and which I have inherited. It's an explosion of colour, form and texture. She actually worked the stitches onto a

above: **My grandmother's spotted cushion, a glorious riot of colour.**

spotted handkerchief and if you look closely you can see the original red printing in between the stitches. All the spots are satin stitch and the rest is a mass of French knots, densely packed together. The colours are truly glorious. It looks as though she threw in every strand of thread she had available. My grandmother was a lovely lady, always beautifully turned out, and I could not imagine her creating anything so riotous, as it didn't go with her silvery-blue rinse and perfectly tied scarves. But there it sits on my sofa, glowing, and I love it.

I like this sense of family history in objects, and when I am working on my own pieces I sometimes wonder where they'll be in years to come. Similarly, I look at samplers in antique shops and wonder about the people who created them, and what sort of lives they might have led. Needlepoint is an intensely personal activity. I can easily lose track of time while stitching, accompanied by the radio. I have to set myself little targets, "I'll just fill in that bit" or "I'll just do another thread", otherwise it starts to get out of hand and I can find myself spending hours absorbed in stitching! I hope that in reading the book you will find projects that inspire you to take up this most satisfying of pastimes. We have tried to provide a wide choice of things to make. Some pieces, like the buttons, you'll be able to complete in an evening or two, and perhaps this will encourage you to try something more demanding. Whatever you try, we hope you'll enjoy making them as much as we enjoyed dreaming them up. **Christine Büttner**

design
inspiration

colour inspiration

Finding inspiration for needlepoint is a matter of keeping your eyes open. There is always something to observe, even in the most unexpected places. Try to make mental notes of what catches your eye, or get into the habit of carrying around a small camera with you and use it as a note book. Or buy a small sketchbook and a box of coloured pencils or pastels and jot down ideas. Colour is often a main trigger for starting a new needlepoint project. Your imagination may be sparked off by the sight of a flower stall on a gray pavement, by variations in paintwork or by intricate architectural details on a building. It is almost impossible to lay down do's and don'ts when it comes to colour selection, as it is such a personal matter. Our personal preferences about what works and what clashes are based on all sorts of influences.

Some people lack confidence when it comes to mixing and matching colours. Some may find choosing and combining colours instinctively easy and others may ponder at length; whatever selection you end up with, certain palettes will appeal to certain people for different reasons. It is rather unwise, I think, to theorize about colour combinations. For instance, you may know the phrase "red and green should never be seen", yet you only have to look at a pot of geraniums in full bloom to realize the vibrancy that these colours can generate together.

Above all, colour should be an unending source of inspiration and experimentation. Feel confident to try all kinds of combinations and decide yourself what your likes and dislikes are. If you feel in need of inspiration, pay a visit to a yarn shop, an art gallery, a bookshop, a beautiful garden or an open-air market. Try keeping a collection of attractive oddments at home for a useful source of reference. For example, collect buttons, labels, matchboxes, scraps of fabric, postcards, magazine cuttings and anything else that catches your attention – one day they might spark off an idea and appear in one of your own needlepoint designs, once you become practised.

It is helpful to sort out yarns according to colour when you are planning a new needlepoint project. If you arrange the threads in a spectrum of red, grading through orange into yellow and then green, turning into blue and purple before coming full circle and merging with red again, then you will have a full palette at your fingertips. Once arranged in this way, you can move the threads around looking for combinations.

The choice of colours available in embroidery threads today is dazzling. The more needlepoint you do, so your collection of yarns will grow and you can experiment more with colour. However, you may convince yourself that you do not have the exact shade that you need and so find a valid reason for making another trip to the yarn shop!

opposite: A detail of my goldfish picture shown on page 41. A visit to a yarn shop will be an inspiration, as the range of yarns available today is enormous. (Christine Büttner)

ethnic influences

Colour is undoubtedly an essential trigger behind creating your own needlepoint designs. However, ethnic arts and crafts provide another rich source of ideas. Tribal and folk art encompass a huge number of styles that have evolved from cultures across the world. In every continent, people have created for centuries, and continue to create, exquisite combinations of pattern and colour from myriad raw materials.

You do not necessarily have to visit museums or art galleries to get a glimpse of the wealth of influences that ethnic customs and traditions may inspire, indeed some of the most extraordindary objects can come to light in everyday situations such as car boot sales, junk or thrift shops, jumble sales and flea markets. Seek out such places and rummage around and sooner or later you will come across objects as diverse as wooden carvings, painted tin, boxes, toys, hand-produced textiles and more. Although you may not wish to purchase any such items, you may be drawn by a particular shape, texture or decoration and so take note of any interesting features. Either make a mental note of what catches your eye, or make a quick sketch, or take a snap with a camera, if you have one to hand. If you get into the habit of scavenging and saving all sorts of attractive oddments then you will have a constant source of reference material for making your own needlepoint designs.

Drawing inspiration from a specific source may be a little more involved than just seeing an object, taking a visual record and transferring it to a canvas for stitching. More often, inspiration will come to you gradually and the whole process becomes an accumulation of ideas that are shuffled and re-shuffled in your mind, then sketched and re-sketched on paper and distilled before materializing as a finished design. Take time to look at an object carefully, whether it is a piece of exquisite fabric or a striking work of art. Try to single out the elements that initially make an impact and use that part as a starting point for creating your own design.

There is a multitude of ethnic objects and artefacts that we can look to for inspiration. You might find a stimulus through travel abroad, or closer to home by hunting through ethnic shops, markets and special exhibitions. Garner ideas from jewellery, baskets, batik, ceramics and tiles, figurines and fabrics. If you wish to give an imaginative gift to someone, then a piece of needlepoint featuring your own original design will be quite unique. For a person who you know to be fond of a particular type of pottery, a style of weaving, the colours and design of an ethnic costume, or the proud owner of a prized possession brought back from far-flung travels, you could take any of these as inspiration and attempt to translate them to needlepoint.

opposite: A detail from my Chinese figures picture on page 50. You can find inspiration from ethnic art, crafts and artefacts in specialist shops, markets and exhibitions. (Caroline Robins)

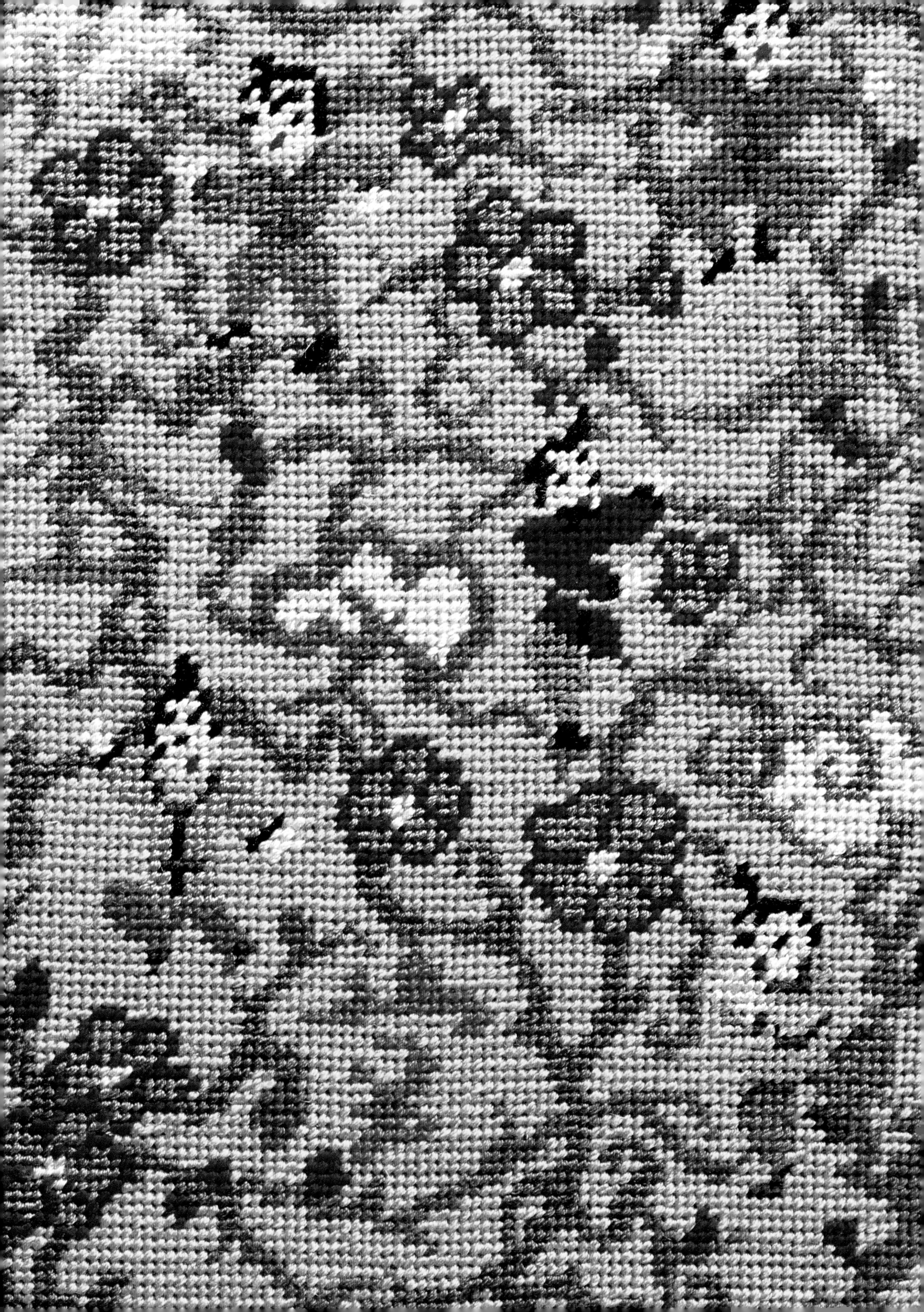

the natural world

Little can surpass the stunning range of colours to be found in the natural world. You have only to take a walk in the open – visit a park in springtime, stroll along a beach during the warm months of the year, observe the glorious hues of foliage as the seasons turn or look to evergreens and berries when other blooms are in short supply, to see the marvellous array of colours that occur in nature. Keep your eyes open and stay alert to your surroundings. Take a cue from nature by having a notebook, sketchbook or a camera to hand to keep a visual record of what you observe around you. Whatever the setting, be it a rugged seascape or a pretty cottage garden, you are sure to discover plenty of stimulus.

The beach is not only a delightful place to walk but a rich hunting ground for ideas. Along the seashore pebbles and shells may catch your eye. Gather up flotsam and jetsam thrown up by the waves and take them home. Later, you can lay the results of your beach combing expedition out on a portable flat surface such as a tray or a wooden board. Move them around until they fall into a pleasing configuration. Then, if you are unable to leave them as arranged for future reference, take a colour photograph of the whole composition to remind you of the layout. You will now have a starting point for creating your own original design. For advice on how to transfer a design to canvas for stitching, see page 139.

A wander through the countryside, whether fields, moorland or woodland, can yield pocketfuls of useful reference material. Look out for gnarled and weathered woodforms, pretty pebbles and shells, interesting foliage and all sorts of wild flowers, nuts and seedheads. Once again, arrange your findings as described and take a photograph or sketch them in position so that you have the basis of a needlepoint design. A holiday is an ideal time to gather a variety of mementos to inspire you. When you have the leisure to enjoy your surroundings to the full, why not attempt to capture them on canvas? You might choose to reflect the tranquillity of a Mediterranean landscape, conjure up the exotic colours of a trip abroad or recreate an image of a favourite animal or family pet in stitches. While abroad, keep a collection of postcards of the local area and take photographs of any usual features, plants or flowers, fruits or vegetables that make an impression; use these different elements to form a visual diary. Keep these recollections and you will find that sifting through them, some may spark off a theme for a needlepoint project. If you wish to translate part or all of a photograph or a postcard into a stitched design, it helps to start with a photocopy of the image. Experiment with the scale of the image using an enlarger facility. You will find it most helpful to make a colour photocopy as a reference for your needlepoint.

opposite: A detail of my tomato placemat design, see page 123. Vegetables, fruit, flowers and much more in the natural world provide all kinds of inspiration for needlepoint design. (Caroline Robins)

textiles & patterns

Because needlepoint is part of the vast textile family, fabric, with its woven construction, is a rich and ready source of inspiration for the would-be needlepoint designer. The intricacies of rich weaves on fabrics such as decorative tapestry, damask or brocade are wonderful to touch and provide plenty of patterns that can be copied or adapted to translate onto canvas.

You may be inspired by some of the stylized architectural motifs that have appeared in classical patterns for hundreds of years. Or you may prefer to play upon the theme of a particular plaid, perhaps choosing a family tartan to cover a cushion or a stool. Then there are the characteristic stripes, circles and blocks of ikat, that are softened because the colours are feathered into each other giving the impression of a kaleidoscope, to consider. Or look to the beautiful ethnic designs of kilims, with their endless configurations of squares and diamonds and sumptuous colours. There is also a wide range of tribal textiles to influence you, from the bold geometrics of a Navaho blanket to the very fine detail of African kente cloth.

Printed fabrics, which are generally used for home furnishing include a vast array of designs from floral chintzes to exotic paisleys, glowing Provençal prints to pastoral *toiles de Jouy*, these exquisite designs are often detailed reproductions of human activities which tell a story.

In addition, the rich, organic patterns of the well-known late 19th-century textile designer and craftsman William Morris are a pure delight. Their subtle colours are achieved by vegetable dyeing and the designs often illustrate stylized depictions of fruit, foliage and flowers, in particular varieties of lily. And applied textiles such as crewelwork, appliqué, patchwork and quilting offer yet more scope for the needlepoint designer. Whether you wish to recreate the decorative feel of an embroidery sampler that you may have seen in an historic house; reproduce the age-old designs of woven tribal or ethnic textiles that your eye was drawn to on a trip overseas; or imitate the vibrancy of a purchased cotton check fabric length, textiles in all their forms provide an almost limitless array of ideas. You can also consider the decorative potential of braids and ribbons; some of these flat woven trimmings are like miniature cloth designs and display glorious attention to detail.

If you like a particular fabric, pick it up and you will notice that by draping the cloth you can form new patterns and rhythms in the design. Another fascinating aspect of fabric that the needlepoint designer should consider is the whole new character that a pattern can take on in a different colourway. Many fabric outlets give away swatches of cloth, so feel free to ask for a cutting to take away as a point of reference.

opposite: A detail of my French cushion that was inspired by various checked fabrics, see page 24. Seek out inspiration from fabric suppliers and take away cuttings. (Christine Büttner)

cushions

TWO CATS CUSHION

This cushion cover was inspired by a photograph of my cats. Brother and sister, they are devoted to each other and often lie like this together, paws and whiskers intertwined, on their favourite napping spot, the sofa.

To make this design, I literally traced the image from the photograph and drew it out onto the canvas from the trace. While I stitched, I kept the picture close by as a reference for shape and colour. Originally, I had intended this project to be a picture to hang above the sofa, and the elongated shape was dictated by an antique pine frame that I had earmarked for it. However, as the piece progressed I had second thoughts and instead decided to make a cushion, envisaging the two cats curled up against it – art reflecting life and vice versa.

The blue and cream plaid motif was based loosely on the sofa fabric I have at home and seemed a natural choice of background for my furry friends. Executing this checked area proved to be a useful way of keeping the tension of the whole piece even. I worked the blue and cream together, so that I had two needles on the go simultaneously. First I plotted out the cream grid lines and then I filled them in with the navy. With all needlepoint it is important to work from the middle of the piece out toward the edges.

I like the idea of framing a stitched piece with a complementary fabric; the textures of the needlepoint and the fabric set each other off well. For this cushion I chose a cream and navy check which echoes the grid pattern of the needlepoint background. You can use a variety of fabrics for this purpose, but you should bear in mind that the weight needs to be similar to that of the stitched panel in order to prevent unsightly puckering at the seams and to ensure that the stitched panel lies flat. I have seen this framing idea used to great effect on patchwork quilts; the stitched panel is rather small compared to the overall size of the quilt and thus looks all the more jewel-like and precious.

If you are feeling adventurous, you could try to develop your own design for a cushion cover or a framed picture. Start with a photograph of your own pet, or else try to search out something appealing on a postcard or in a magazine. Try too to devise your own background pattern so that the cushion will relate to your furnishings. Repeat patterns are a satisfying way of filling in a large area of canvas. If you feel nervous about designing one yourself, then visit your local fabric shop for ideas. There is no need to tackle anything too complicated; often simple designs are the most effective.

opposite: My two cats – Big Boy, a gloriously handsome but dim tabby, and Stripe, his eccentric-looking but intelligent sister – recreated in stitches. (Christine Büttner)

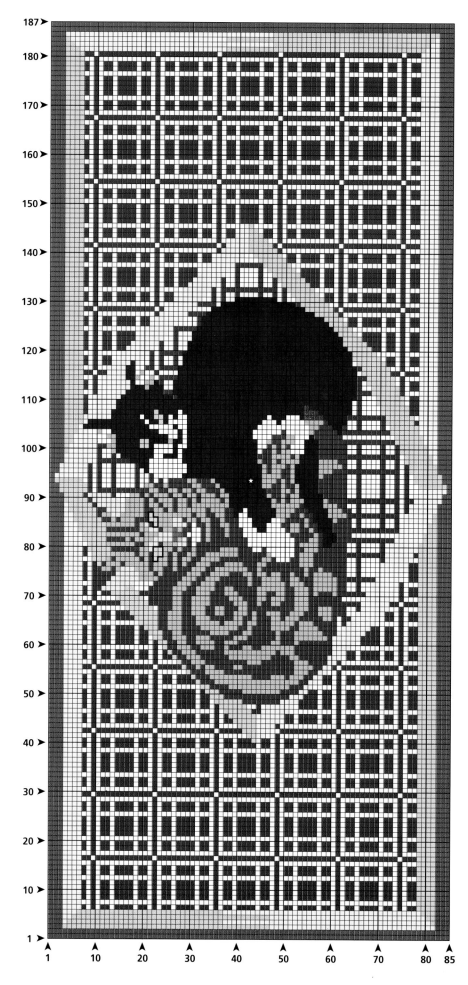

Use Anchor stranded cotton in the colours and quantities in the key below. The initial numbers refer to the Anchor codes; the numbers that follow in brackets refer to the number of skeins required. An 8 m (9 yd) skein will work approximately 1,150 stitches. (For DMC equivalents, see the conversion chart on page 140.)

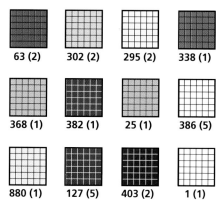

63 (2)	302 (2)	295 (2)	338 (1)
368 (1)	382 (1)	25 (1)	386 (5)
880 (1)	127 (5)	403 (2)	1 (1)

☆ Mid-point of design

— Backstitch in 382

MATERIALS & EQUIPMENT

16-gauge canvas, 40 x 23 cm (16 x 9 in)

40 cm (½ yd) of 122 cm (48 in) wide

fabric for backing and borders

Medium-weight fabric 37 x 48 cm

(15 x 18 ¾ in) for lining front cover

Strong thread to match backing fabric

Cushion pad 35 x 45 cm (14 x 18 in)

Size 22 tapestry needle

Measures about 35 x 46 cm (14 x 18 in)

Use all six strands of thread for stitching

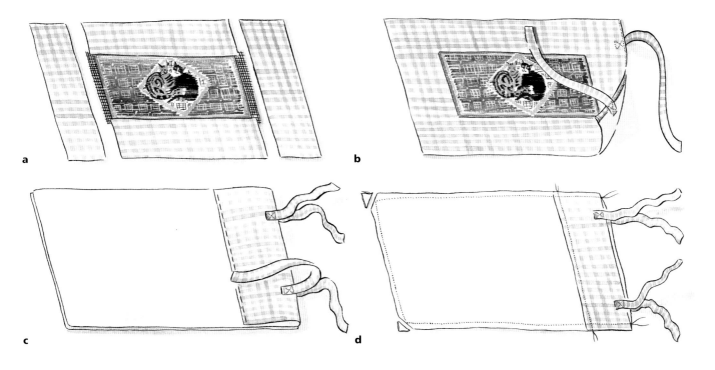

a

b

c

d

Making up instructions

1 First block the completed needlepoint (see page 136). Trim the outer edges of the canvas to 2 cm (¾ in) all around.

2 From the backing fabric, cut out one rectangle for the back, 37 x 55 cm (15 x 22 in); two rectangles for the top and bottom borders, each one 13 x 31.5 cm (5 x 12¼ in); two rectangles for the side borders, each one 10.5 x 37 cm (4 x 15 in); four strips for the ties, each one 37 x 6 cm (15 x 2½ in).

3 Place the needlepoint right side up and pin the top border piece right side down over it so the fabric overlaps the edges by 1 cm (⅜ in) along the top and side edges (a). Pin, baste and stitch the pieces together, stitch just inside the edge of the needlepoint to stop the canvas threads showing. Repeat to join the bottom border piece to the lower edge of the needlepoint. Open out both border pieces and press the seams.

4 In the same way, join the side border pieces to the needlepoint and to the top and bottom borders, again taking 1 cm (⅜ in) seam allowance. Press.

5 Turn under the edge of the right-hand border to make a double 5 mm (¼ in) hem. Machine stitch or slipstitch the hem (see Techniques, page 138).

6 Make a narrow hem on one short side of the back piece. Turn this edge under a further 8 cm (3 in). Press.

7 Make the ties. Fold each strip in half lengthways. Machine stitch along the long edges of the strip and across one short end, taking 1 cm (⅜ in) seam allowance. Trim the corners diagonally to reduce bulk, then turn the strip right side out. (A knitting needle or tweezers will be helpful here.)

8 Pin two ties to the front cover, just underneath the hemmed edge. Hand sew the ties on the wrong side (b).

9 Make a narrow hem on one short edge of the lining fabric. Lay the front cover wrong side up and place the lining on top. Make sure that all of the edges are aligned. Pin and baste around the edges. Slipstitch the hemmed side edges together (see Techniques, page 138).

10 Place the back and front cover right sides facing. Position the remaining ties on the turned-back edge; align them with the front ties. Hand sew them neatly and securely in place, stitching through the folded-back fabric only (c).

11 Pin together the back and front sections of the cushion around three edges, leaving the short edges with the ties open. Baste and stitch together (d). Trim the corners diagonally to reduce bulk and turn the cover right side out. Press the edges with the point of an iron. Insert the cushion pad and tie the bows to close the cover.

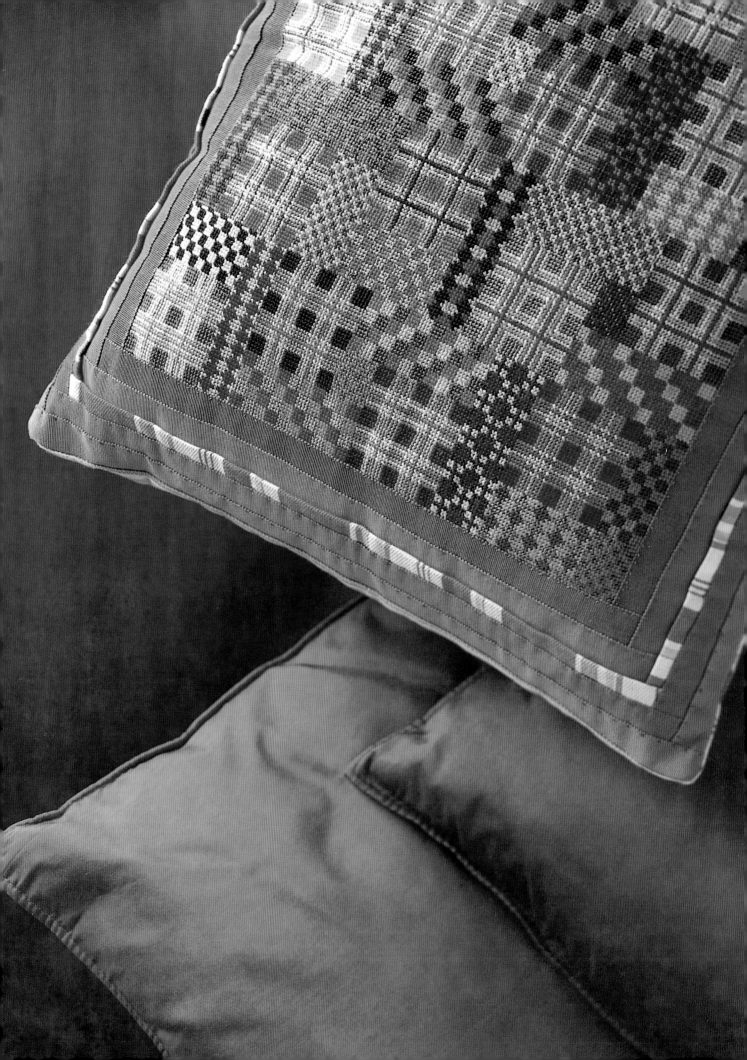

FRENCH CUSHION

I love this cushion; it's full of memories of a glorious Easter I spent with my good friend Jean in France. During a few cold, wet days we sat indoors, fortified by mugs of tea and stitched away happily. Inspired by the recent revival of tartans that appeared on the cat-walks and in interior decoration, where shocking colour combinations were being thrown together with cheerful irreverence, I was enticed to have a go myself and so began experimenting with all sorts of plaids and checks. The piece finally took off when I decided to do a sampler of all the various combinations that I wished to try out.

Needlepoint lends itself beautifully to this type of grid-based design. In essence, what you have to do is carefully count the squares of the canvas and keep to horizontal, verti-cal or diagonal straight lines. I hadn't planned the design in any great detail before I started and the only parameters that I imposed upon myself were to use a limited number of basic block designs – six in all – and to maintain a visual rhythm within the main tartan blocks. Everything else would fall into place and the colours would work their own special magic. In addition, I tried to limit the size of the individual blocks so that I would not get bored stitching any one part of the design.

In this way, the piece developed into an exciting exercise using tone and colour. By simply changing the combinations and emphasis of light and dark, hot and cool colours, I was able to alter dramatically the balance within each block. For example, in the deep blue tartan the strongest elements are the dark blue squares with the pink and yellow lines glowing between them; the effect brings to mind memories of fireworks against a night sky. By contrast, in the pink and green tartan, the blue and green dividers leap out from the pink.

You can experiment endlessly with the effects that colours have on each other. One of the most exciting, though sometimes rather frustrating, aspects of working on this piece was actually settling on which colours to mix together: the brilliant oranges next to the startling blues; strawberry pinks and yellows offset by purple; shocking reds singing out against emerald green and so on. I spent many hours experimenting with different colour combinations, feeling some-thing like an alchemist striving for the perfect mix of ingredients.

I chose to work my French cushion in stranded cotton on a relatively fine canvas, in order to give the finished piece a jewel-like, luminous quality.

opposite: A vibrant cushion inspired by myriad tartans, checks and plaids. The design is created on a grid pattern and was stitched on a holiday in France. (Christine Büttner)

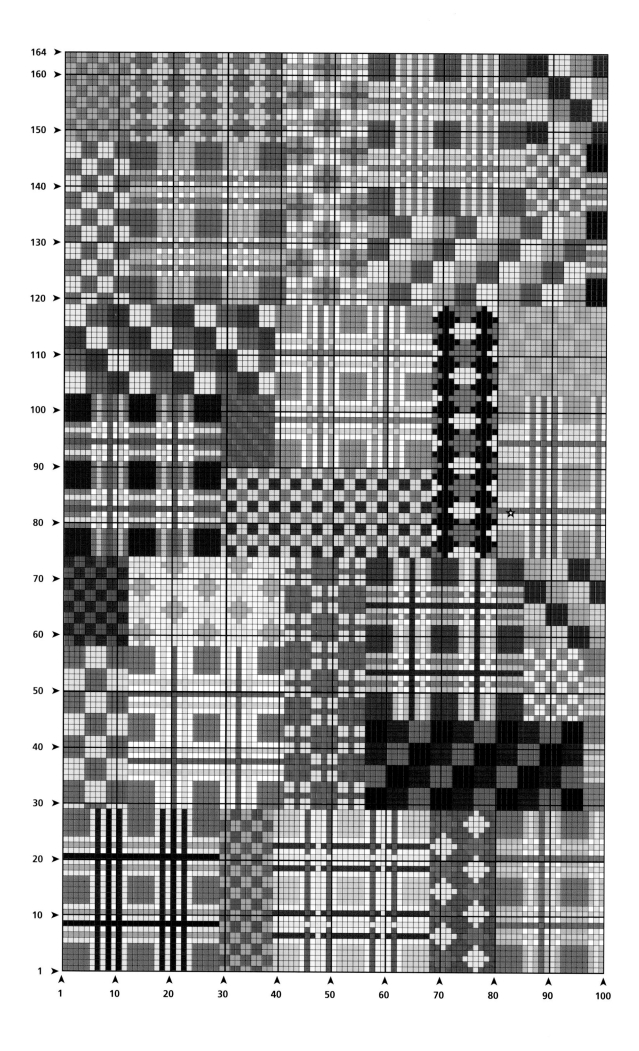

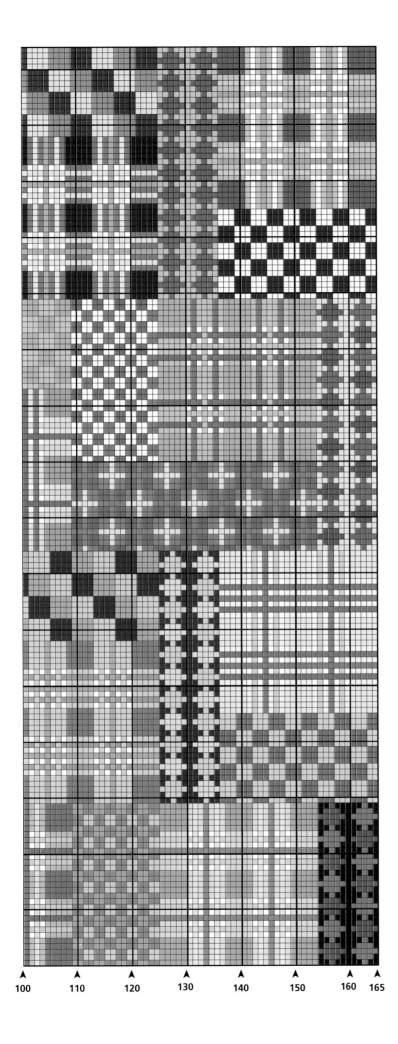

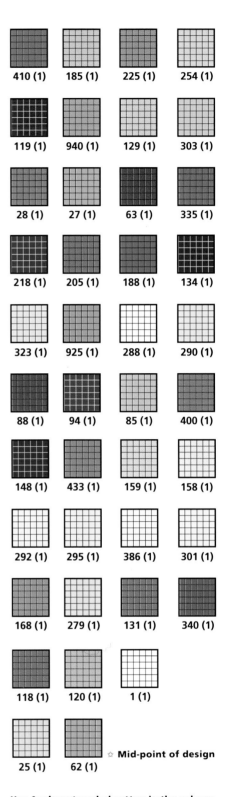

410 (1)	185 (1)	225 (1)	254 (1)
119 (1)	940 (1)	129 (1)	303 (1)
28 (1)	27 (1)	63 (1)	335 (1)
218 (1)	205 (1)	188 (1)	134 (1)
323 (1)	925 (1)	288 (1)	290 (1)
88 (1)	94 (1)	85 (1)	400 (1)
148 (1)	433 (1)	159 (1)	158 (1)
292 (1)	295 (1)	386 (1)	301 (1)
168 (1)	279 (1)	131 (1)	340 (1)
118 (1)	120 (1)	1 (1)	
25 (1)	62 (1)		

☆ Mid-point of design

100   110   120   130   140   150   160   165

Use Anchor stranded cotton in the colours and quantities in the key above. The initial numbers refer to the Anchor codes; the numbers that follow in brackets refer to the number of skeins required. An 8 m (9 yd) skein will work about 1,150 stitches. (For DMC equivalents, see the conversion chart on page 140.)

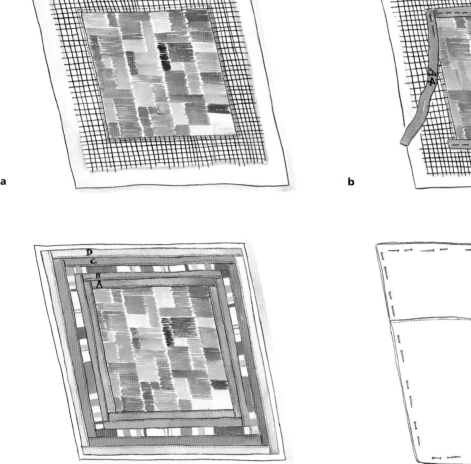

a

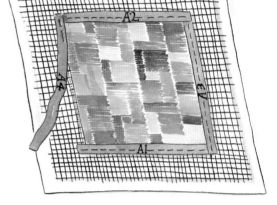

b

c

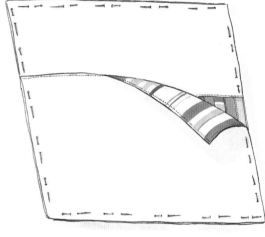

d

MATERIALS & EQUIPMENT

16-gauge canvas, 36 cm (14 in) square

Soft cotton fabric, 42 cm (16½ in) square
for lining the front cover

50 cm (½ yd) of medium-weight striped
cotton fabric for backing and trimming

Four different-coloured ribbons, each
2 cm (¾ in) wide, in the following
quantities: ribbon A, 1.3 m (1⅜ yd);
ribbon B, 1.5 m (1⅝ in) wide; ribbon C, 1.7 cm

(1⅞ yd); ribbon D, 1.7 m (1⅞ yd)

Coloured sewing threads to contrast with
the ribbons

Size 22 tapestry needle

The finished needlepoint measures
approximately 27 cm (10½ in) square; the
cushion measures approximately 40 cm
(16 in) square

Use all six strands of thread for stitching

I designed my colourful French cushion
using several closely related shades,
which are difficult to distinguish on the
chart (see previous page). Don't worry
too much about using the "correct" shade
in every case; feel free to improvise.

Making up instructions

1 First block or stretch the completed needlepoint. Have this done by a professional or follow the instructions on page 136. Trim off the outer edges of the canvas where the tacks were inserted during the blocking, in order to leave the edges of the canvas smooth on all sides.

2 From the medium-weight striped cotton fabric for the backing, cut out two separate pieces, each one should measure 42 x 25 cm (16½ x 10 in). Then cut out four strips of striped fabric, each one should measure 3 cm (1¼ in) wide and 37 cm (14½ in) long. Make sure that you cut out these strips across the fabric so that the stripes will all run correctly and fall parallel with the border. When cutting out it is best to err on the generous side; you can always trim away excess fabric later.

3 Place the square piece of lining fabric (ideally this should be a soft cotton) on a flat, smooth surface and lay the needlepoint on top of it, centre it exactly; it should be 7.5 cm (3 in) in from each edge. Pin it in position around all four edges; then you should re-check the measurements and adjust the position of the needlepoint if necessary. Baste the two layers together and then machine stitch them, following the edges of the needlepoint (a). If you do not have a sewing machine to hand, then you can sew the seams by hand using backstitch (see Techniques, page 137.)

4 From ribbon A cut out four lengths, each one should be 31 cm (12¼ in) long. Position two of these (called A1 and A2 on the illustration shown left) on two opposite sides

of the needlepoint, with the two ends extending approximately 2 cm (¾ in) beyond it. Pin and baste the ribbons in place. Position the other two pieces (A3 and A4 on the illustration shown left) along the adjacent sides, with the ends overlapping A1 and A2. Baste them in place (b).

5 From ribbon B, cut out a strip the length of A1 plus 4 cm (1½ in). Note that it is better to cut this and the following ribbons in relation to the previous round of ribbons, in order to allow for any slight variations that may occur as the work proceeds. Position this strip so that it overlaps strip A1 by approximately 5 mm (¼ in) and extends about 2 cm (¾ in) beyond each end. Pin and baste the strips together, for the distance of the needlepoint only, so as to avoid concealing the ends of the basting under the ends of the adjacent ribbons. Carefully measure, then cut out and position the remaining strips of B in the same way as before.

6 Fold each fabric strip in half lengthways, with the wrong sides together. Press with the point of an iron. (The fabric strips are intentionally narrower than the ribbons because of their strong pattern, which would otherwise be rather too intrusive. Note that the needlepoint should be the most prominent part of the cushion design, in spite of the bold border.) Position the strips of fabric in the same sequence as you have already established for the ribbons, (to help you to do this, turn back to the photograph on page 24 for reference). Overlap the B ribbons by approximately 5 mm (¼ in). Pin and then baste the strips in

position. Trim the ends if necessary so that they just overlap each other.

7 Apply ribbons C and D in the same way as before, overlapping the raw edges of the fabric strips again by 5 mm (¼ in). The outer edges of the D ribbons should be about 5 mm (¼ in) from the edges of the lining fabric, so that they will be caught into the 1 cm (⅜ in) seam, and the corners of the ribbon border should line up with the corner of the lining fabric. You may need to adjust the positions of the ribbons slightly in order to achieve this.

8 Using your chosen contrasting coloured sewing threads and with a neat, tiny running stitch, sew the ribbons securely in place along their inner edges. The hand stitching that you make on ribbon C will also help to secure the fabric strip (c).

9 On each of the two back cover pieces turn under 1 cm (⅜ in) along one long edge. Machine stitch the hem in place, or use backstitch (see Techniques, page 137). Press the hem with the point of an iron.

10 Lay the front cover fabric right side up on a flat surface and place the two back cover pieces on top of it. Overlap the hemmed edges and align all four raw edges around the sides. Pin and baste the front and back of the cushion together in position (d). Machine stitch (or backstitch) around all the edges, taking a 1 cm (⅜ in) seam. Press the seams flat with an iron.

11 Trim off all four corners diagonally outside the seam in order to reduce bulk, and turn the cushion cover right side out. Press once again with an iron. The final step is to insert the cushion pad.

TARTAN CUSHION

Being a proud Scot, tartans are part of my childhood memories and I have always been fond of tartan kilts, rugs and furnishings.

I thought it would be fun to work some tartan in needlepoint and felt that the designs could be translated onto canvas with little difficulty and that the colour combinations would be most attractive. At the same time, I was keen to give my friends Leaf and Jo a special wedding gift and this seemed the ideal opportunity to try a tartan design. A cushion seemed appropriate and the rich colours of this MacPherson tartan were suitably joyous. What an easy and pleasurable project it turned out to be! And it was not without surprises either. For example, it is hard to believe that this cushion consists of just seven different shades of yarn, but by intermingling the colours the pattern creates an impression of many more.

As I worked on this cushion I began to realize that I had stumbled upon a design idea that would appeal to other needlepoint enthusiasts, especially those who prefer to see rapid results. Sometimes, when I ask why someone has abandoned a project, the answer is because of the slow progress of the work and the feeling that hours of stitching do not speedily yield a completed project. If you too get discouraged for this reason, then a tartan cushion could be just the project to help revive your flagging spirits. You should find that you cover the canvas reasonably fast, and, because the design is not complicated and relies on pattern repeats, the project will also suit beginners.

As an alternative to this exact design you might like to change the combinations of the colours, or you could choose a different tartan altogether – perhaps your own family one, if you have Scottish ancestry. There are some wonderful books to inspire you. My own source of reference for this cushion was *The Clans and Tartans of Scotland* by Robert Bains, which I found in the local library. You could also select a tartan from a fabric retail outlet and you only need to purchase one pattern repeat. Another idea is to take a tartan rug and make a needlepoint cushion to match. Or, you might like to take just a small section of this cushion and repeat it; this will simplify the design and make the whole easier and quicker to execute. Whatever you eventually decide on, do not worry if you do not follow the chart overleaf exactly; small mistakes will not detract from the overall impression. All you have to do is start stitching, let the tartan grow and enjoy the satisfaction of watching the bare canvas quickly disappear!

opposite: The rich colours of the MacPherson tartan were the inspiration behind this cushion, which was made as a wedding gift. (Caroline Robins)

ght side out.
n pad, then slip-
page 138) the
er, leaving a gap of
1 in).
aid to the outer edges of
place one end into the gap
with a few hand stitches (c).
wing the braid along the seam
and secure hand stitches.
you reach the point where you
ed the braid, trim the end of the
d, leaving about 2 cm (¾ in). Insert this
nd into the gap and secure it with a few
hand stitches; try to sew any remaining gap in the
ble (d). Sew up any remaining gap in the
seam with slipstitch. (To prevent the braid
ends from fraying you can wrap a piece of
sticky tape around them.)

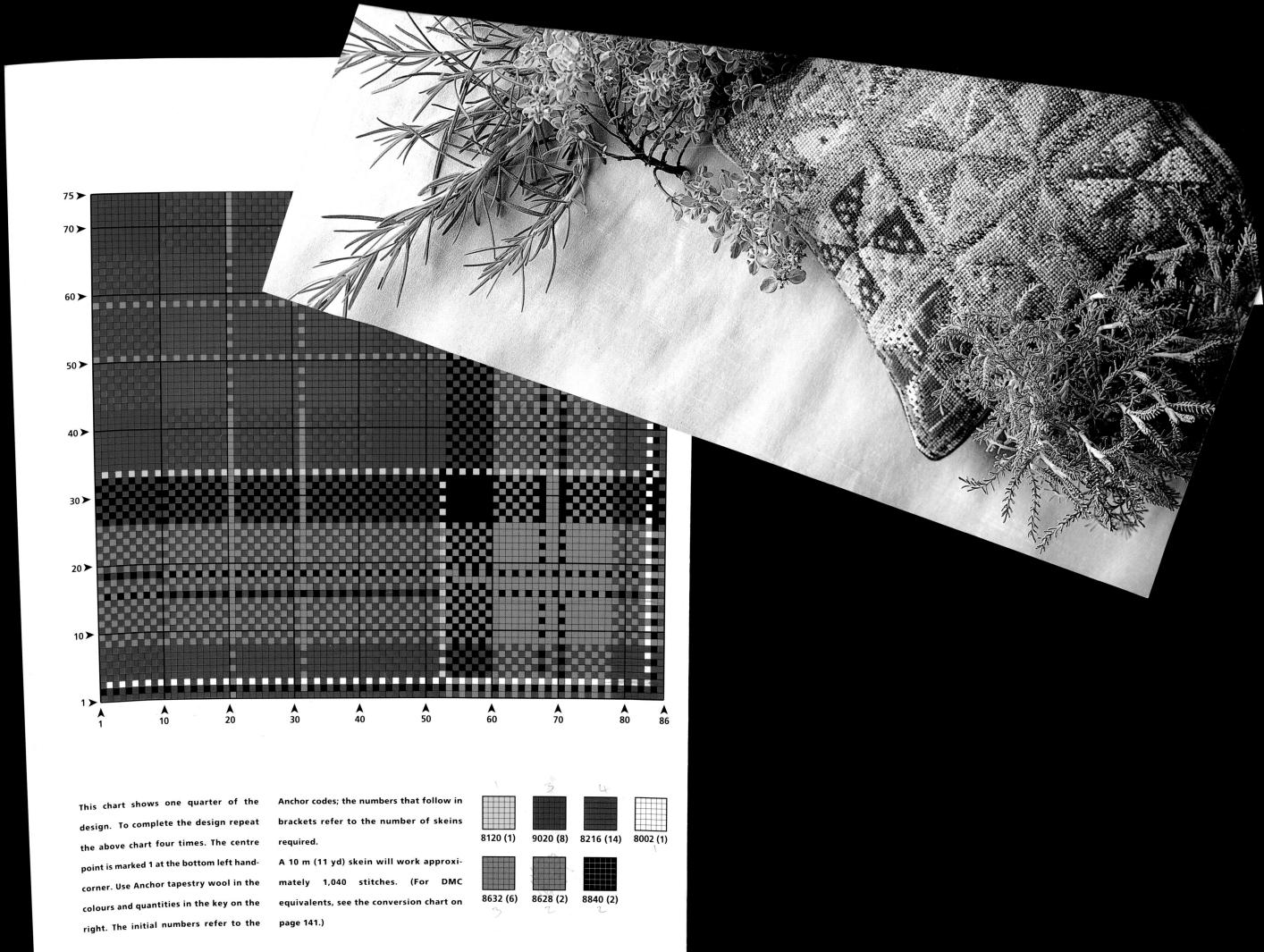

This chart shows one quarter of the design. To complete the design repeat the above chart four times. The centre point is marked 1 at the bottom left hand-corner. Use Anchor tapestry wool in the colours and quantities in the key on the right. The initial numbers refer to the Anchor codes; the numbers that follow in brackets refer to the number of skeins required.

A 10 m (11 yd) skein will work approximately 1,040 stitches. (For DMC equivalents, see the conversion chart on page 141.)

8120 (1)   9020 (8)   8216 (14)   8002 (1)

8632 (6)   8628 (2)   8840 (2)

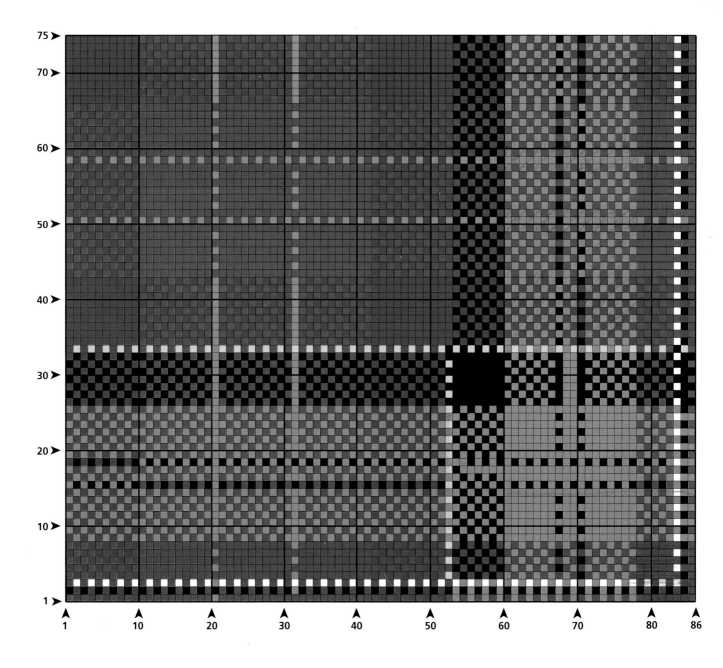

This chart shows one quarter of the design. To complete the design repeat the above chart four times. The centre point is marked 1 at the bottom left hand-corner. Use Anchor tapestry wool in the colours and quantities in the key on the right. The initial numbers refer to the

Anchor codes; the numbers that follow in brackets refer to the number of skeins required.

A 10 m (11 yd) skein will work approximately 1,040 stitches. (For DMC equivalents, see the conversion chart on page 141.)

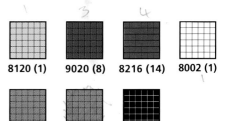

8120 (1)   9020 (8)   8216 (14)   8002 (1)

8632 (6)   8628 (2)   8840 (2)

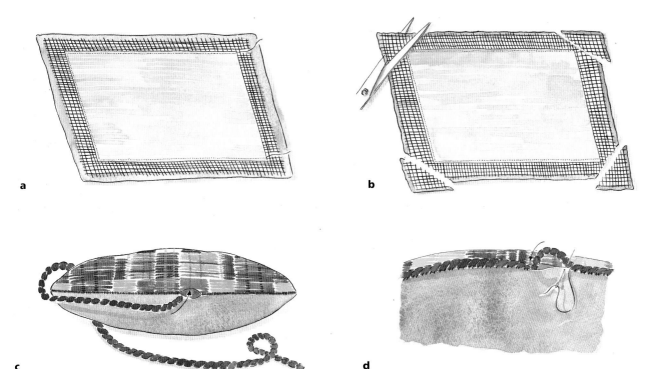

a

b

c

d

MATERIALS & EQUIPMENT

13-gauge canvas, 40 x 50 cm (16 x 20 in)

Furnishing fabric for backing,

34 x 44 cm (13½ x 17½ in)

1.5 m (1⅝ yd) of furnishing braid

Cushion pad, 30 x 40 cm (12 x 16 in)

Strong sewing thread to match backing

fabric and braid

Size 18 tapestry needle

Measures 29 x 30 cm (11½ x 13 in)

Use one strand of thread for stitching

Making up instructions

1 First block or stretch the needlepoint. I recommend that you have this done by a professional. However, if you wish to do this yourself at home, then follow the instructions given in the Techniques section on page 136. Trim the outer canvas edges to 2 cm (¾ in) all around.

2 Place the piece of backing fabric on the needlepoint with right sides facing. Pin and baste the two pieces together around three edges, then machine stitch the layers together, leaving one side open (a). You can use backstitch (see Techniques, page 137) as an alternative to machine stitching. Work the stitching just inside the needlepoint in order to prevent any bare canvas threads from showing. Trim off the four corners diagonally to reduce bulk (b).

3 Turn the cushion cover right side out. Insert the purchased cushion pad, then slipstitch (see Techniques, page 138) the opening edges together, leaving a gap of approximately 3 cm (1 in).

4 To attach the braid to the outer edges of the cushion, first place one end into the gap and secure it with a few hand stitches (c). Continue sewing the braid along the seam with neat and secure hand stitches.

When you reach the point where you inserted the braid, trim the end of the braid, leaving about 2 cm (¾ in). Insert this end into the gap and secure it with a few hand stitches; try to sew as neatly as possible (d). Sew up any remaining gap in the seam with slipstitch. (To prevent the braid ends from fraying you can wrap a piece of sticky tape around them.)

PATCHWORK CUSHION

I greatly admire the skill involved in patchwork and I find it a fascinating craft. Patchwork quilts are wonderful works of art, often with considerable historical value. I am amazed at how their designs manage to appear relevant and quite in keeping with today's interiors, no matter how old they may be. Nowadays, contemporary artists, inspired by the expressive qualities of this old craft, continue to create all kinds of stunning quilts with modern designs that are worked by hand and by machine.

During the 18th and 19th centuries patchwork was an important means of recycling fabric, as well as an outlet for women to produce creative needlework. Quilts were essential furnishings and every young woman aimed to have several in her hope chest by the time she was married. When a quilt top had been pieced, friends gathered together to work the quilt in so-called quilting "bees" and so gave the craft an added social dimension. Among some very devout communities there was a belief that because only God was perfect it was irreverent for a human to produce a perfect object. Therefore it was obligatory to make one deliberate mistake in each quilt, such as an upside-down motif or part of the design cut out from the wrong colour.

I was inspired to adapt a quilt design and see how it would look when interpreted in needlepoint. Some patchwork patterns are highly complicated, but I found the 19th-century Pennsylvanian Pinwheel block served my purpose. It has a lively quality and lots of movement. I chose an 18-gauge canvas to allow for the fine detail I wanted.

This project will help you to learn to use subtle tones and create delicate shading. Once completed, you will have a beautifully intricate piece of work to take great pride in and one which would make a fine gift. This cushion would look particularly at home placed on a patchwork quilt, if you are lucky enough to possess one.

When you make up the cushion take care to select a backing fabric that complements the needlepoint colours. In this case, I found some Austrian cotton in just the right shade of brown. If your own remnants collection contains nothing suitable then try the remnant counter of a fabric shop. For the fastening ribbon at the back of the cushion (which is not visible in the photograph) I chose thin strips of contrasting burgundy shade relating to the overall design. Because the cushion is small I had to make the pad for it myself; to do this I used soft cotton fabric and a polyester fibrefill.

opposite: The Pinwheel patchwork pattern prompted this cushion design, which is full of movement and shows subtle gradations of colour. (Caroline Robins)

CUSHIONS

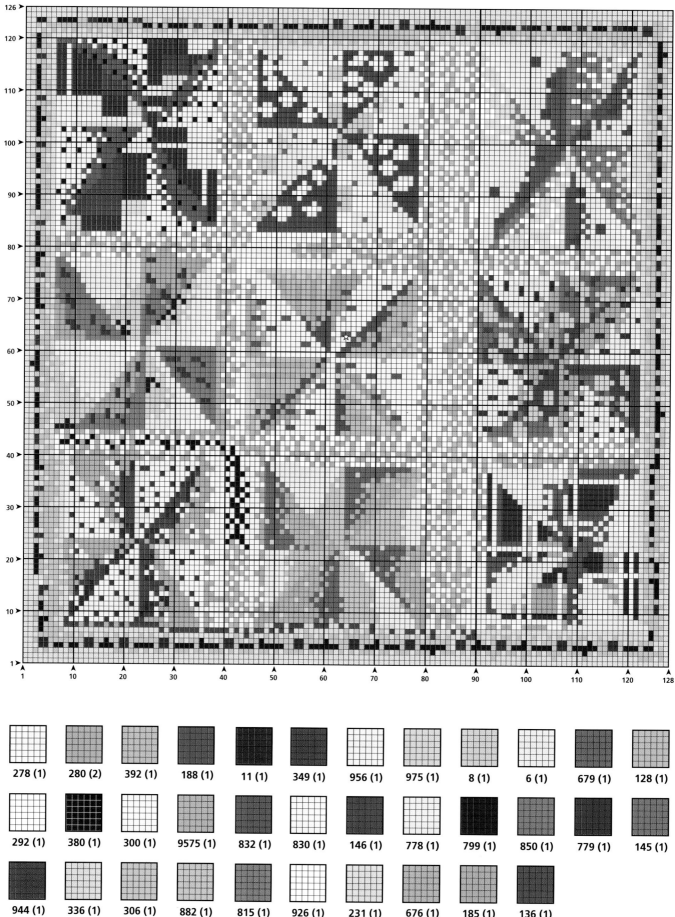

278 (1)   280 (2)   392 (1)   188 (1)   11 (1)   349 (1)   956 (1)   975 (1)   8 (1)   6 (1)   679 (1)   128 (1)

292 (1)   380 (1)   300 (1)   9575 (1)   832 (1)   830 (1)   146 (1)   778 (1)   799 (1)   850 (1)   779 (1)   145 (1)

944 (1)   336 (1)   306 (1)   882 (1)   815 (1)   926 (1)   231 (1)   676 (1)   185 (1)   136 (1)

PATCHWORK CUSHION

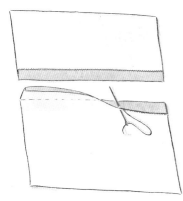

a

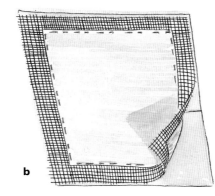

b

c

☆ **Mid-point of design**

Use Anchor stranded cotton in the colours and quantities given in the key opposite. The initial numbers refer to the Anchor yanrs; the numbers that follow in brackets refer to the number of skeins required. An 8 m (9 yd) skein will work approximately 1,450 stitches. (For DMC equivalents, see the conversion chart on page 140.)

MATERIALS & EQUIPMENT

18-gauge canvas, 28 cm (11 in) square

Backing fabric, 26 x 22 cm (10 x 8½ in) square for lining the front cover

2 lengths of coloured ribbon, each 3 mm (⅛ in) wide and 80 cm (⅞ yd) long

Plain cotton fabric for cushion pad, 20 x 40 cm (8 x 16 in)

Polyester filling

Size 20 tapestry needle

Measures 18 cm (7 in) square

Use all six strands of thread for stitching

Making up instructions

1 First block or stretch the finished piece of needlepoint. I recommend that you have this done by a professional. However, if you wish to do this yourself at home, then you should follow the instructions given in the Techniques section on page 136. Trim the outer canvas edges to 2 cm (¾ in) all around.

2 Because of the small size of this cushion you may not be able to buy a ready-made pad. However, it is quite simple to make your own cushion pad, for this project or for any of the previous cushion projects. To make the pad, cut the plain cotton fabric into two pieces, each one should measure 20 cm (8 in) square. Place the two pieces of cotton right sides facing and stitch around three sides, taking a 2 cm (¾ in) seam allowance. You can stitch by machine, or use backstitch (see Techniques, page 137). When you have finished stitching, turn the pad right side out and fill it (not too firmly) with polyester filling. Stitch along the remaining side in order to close it. (Since the cushion pad will not be visible, it is acceptable to leave the seam allowances on the outside, as was done here.)

3 Cut the piece of backing fabric across the width, approximately 10 cm (4 in) down from one edge. Turn under 5 mm (¼ in) then 1.5 cm (½ in) on each of the cut edges to form a neat double hem and stitch these hems in place (a).

4 Place the two hemmed backing pieces together on a flat surface, with right sides upward and the two hemmed edges touching. Place the trimmed needlepoint on top, right side down and pin it to the backing pieces all around the edge of the stitching (b). Baste the two layers together and then machine stitch around all four sides, just inside the stitched area. As an alternative to machine stitching you can use backstitch (see Techniques, page 137). Trim off the four corners outside the seam lines diagonally in order to reduce bulk. Then turn the cushion cover right side out.

5 Cut the two lengths of ribbon in half and sew one half of each pair to the inner hemmed edges of the backing, at a point approximately 5 cm (2 in) in from each side edge (c). Insert the cushion pad into the case and tie the lengths of ribbon into bows to fasten the cover.

pictures

GOLDFISH PICTURE

I call this my goldfish picture. It is based on a painting by Henri Matisse which shows a goldfish bowl and its inhabitants on a table. However, I have adapted it and replaced the original background of flora and fauna with some of my own favourite objects. The background pattern of a dove and balustrade is based on my sofa fabric, which is a gloriously flamboyant design called "Côte d'Azur". In sharp contrast, the geometric black and white tabletop was derived from the tiling around the fireplace in my living room. Around the fish bowl I have placed various presents that close friends have given me – a nest of Russian dolls from St Petersburg, a tiny mask from Indonesia and a painted wooden fish from some forgotten locale. I have used some artistic licence in depicting these items, and just as objects often appear fragmented when seen through a goldfish bowl, I have altered the scale of the objects so that they sit together well in the composition; playing with the scale also allowed me to stitch the smaller items in some detail. Another much-loved object that features in this picture is the cushion cover made by my grandmother (see page 7). The design consists of hundreds of French knots densely worked in satin stitch, and was inspired by a man's spotted handkerchief.

I enjoy creating this sort of personal still-life picture in needlepoint, as the end result relates directly to a person, their surroundings and belongings. For this reason, this kind of composition makes a particularly special gift. If you feel like the challenge of tackling a similar piece of work then start by constructing a still-life on a reasonably small and manageable scale. For ideas as to the treatment you could look in a local card shop or visit an art gallery and take a close look at the composition and use of colour in still-life paintings. Once you have settled on a pleasing arrangement, assemble the items that you wish to incorporate into your image, for instance flowers and plants, fabrics and ornaments can all serve as subject matter. Do not worry unduly about perspective or attempt to recreate precise shadings. Instead, it is much easier to take a two-dimensional, graphic approach rather than a photo-realistic one. Be bold! After all, you are creating a piece that will be personal and you should make it as dynamic and visually interesting as possible – and have some fun in the process. The finished piece could be made into a cushion cover, used to upholster a stool or simply framed, protected behind glass, and hung on the wall in a place where it will look at home.

opposite: Inspired by a painting by Henri Matisse, I created my own Goldfish picture
which includes some of my favourite possessions. (Christine Büttner)

above: A needlepoint picture depicting some of the contents in a friends' home. (Christine Büttner)

Two friends of mine asked me to compose a needlepoint picture for them inspired by their home. So, armed with my camera and a notebook I paid them a visit. I was so struck by the dizzy array of strong colours I felt that the finished picture should reflect this.

All kinds of elements grabbed my attention. The outer border is copied from the fabric of the kitchen blind, which I broke into graphic blocks to use as a repeat pattern. The black and white design is from the tiling in the bathroom and the squares of primary colours are lifted from the shower curtain. The vibrant background in the middle, with its lively black dots and squiggles was based on a pair of summer shorts. The blue, green and red segment peeping out from behind the window pane was the kitchen clock and the placid-looking duck a doorstop. The window frame is taken from the bathroom and the two gray shadows with the lime-green eyes represent two cats. A third cat creeps into the picture on the right-hand side but this is a wooden carved and painted one. The lightbulb depicts a huge lamp which lies on the floor and I represented it switched on for impact. Since I finished the piece my friends have moved house, but most of the objects in the picture are still with them.

I made this picture as a gift for a friend and I wanted to create an image that would be a reflection of her life. I chose her kitchen window as a framework and then built around this with other favourite objects. Mina's green fingers and love of gardening are shown in the plants within the window panes. On the windowsill I assembled some of her possessions – a wooden mask, Indian printing blocks, a painted Russian tea caddy, a nest of dolls, a teapot, a decoy duck and a torch in the shape of the one held by the Statue of Liberty. This reminder of New York was intentional as Mina has worked there and loves the city. The shards of light that radiate from the pendulum lamp echo the painting "Guernica", by Picasso – an artist Mina much admires. If you look at the middle of the rose you will see a copyright symbol which refers to the BBC's "Late Show", on which Mina works. This is definitely a picture for her and no-one else.

above: Designed for my friend Mina, this picture captures aspects of her life and work. (Christine Büttner)

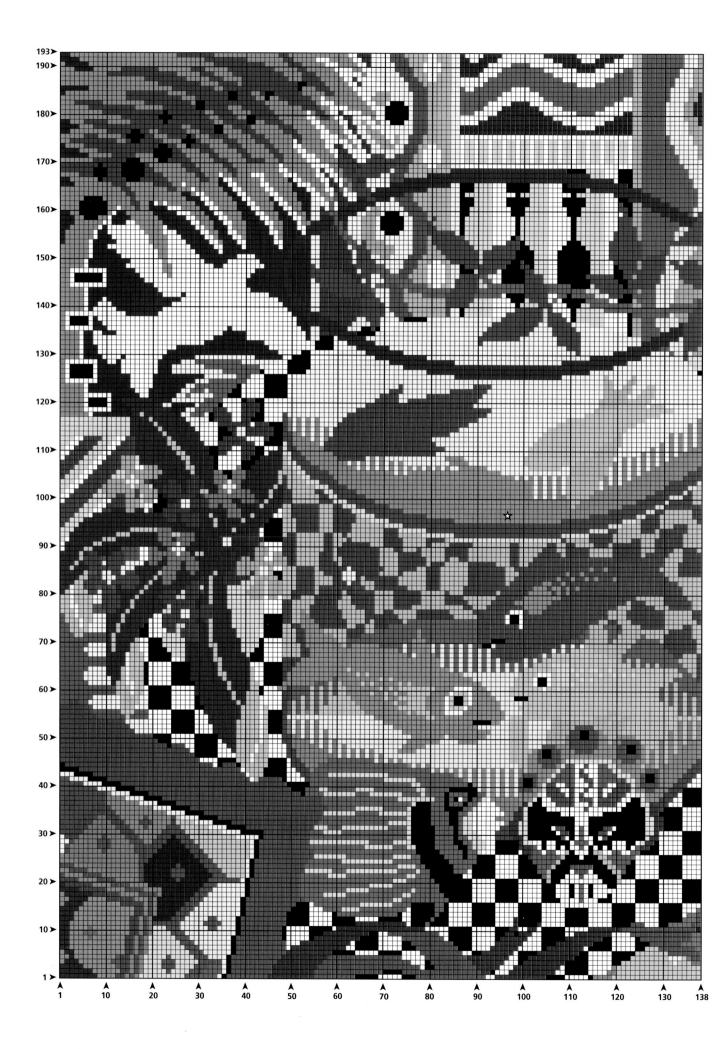

8692 (3)	8986 (2)	8922 (3)	8808 (3)
8688 (3)	8610 (3)	8612 (3)	8694 (3)
8690 (3)	9028 (3)	8964 (3)	8920 (3)
9116 (3)	9092 (3)	8990 (3)	9118 (3)
9012 (3)	8114 (3)	8118 (3)	8116 (3)
8092 (3)	8232 (3)	8124 (3)	8168 (3)
8200 (8)	8440 (3)	8204 (3)	8416 (3)
8436 (3)	8458 (3)	8714 (4)	9798 (3)
8036 (3)	8292 (9)	9496 (1)	9800 (11)

☆ **Mid-point of design**

Use Anchor wool in the colours and quantities in the key above. The initial numbers refer to the Anchor yarns; the numbers that follow in brackets refer to the number of skeins required. A 10 m (11 yd) skein will work about 300 stitches. (For DMC equivalents, see the conversion chart on page 141.)

MATERIALS & EQUIPMENT

7-gauge canvas, 80 cm (32 in) square

Size 16 tapestry needle

Picture frame

The finished picture measures

65 cm (26 in) square

Use two strands of threads for stitching

ALPHABET PICTURE

Typography and lettering tend to be somewhat underrated forms of art and design. This may be because we are surrounded by print every day. Whether on billboards, on packaging, in magazines, newspapers or books, our lives are full of the printed word. Good typography is taken very much for granted, but a slight mistake or misalignment offend the eye immediately.

Ever since I was a child I have loved letterforms. My father was a graphic designer and from an early age I would visit him in his studio and spend hours poring over his books of type samples, unable to believe that the alphabet could exist in such a staggering number of variations. Just as it fascinated me then, so I still get a thrill in seeing an eye-catching piece of typographical design.

In this project I succeeded in combining two of my great loves – lettering and needlepoint. The original idea behind this picture was to create a contemporary version of a sampler. As I began to work on the design I started combining groups of letters to make new, abstract forms. These groups gradually grew and linked up and so the design took off. The colours were inspired by a piece of fabric that I spotted in a market, which juxtaposed strong ruby red, black and gray. I thought that it would be intriguing to examine the positive-negative aspect of the shapes, in other words the spaces inside and in-between them. To do this I placed a frame in the middle of the image and decided that all the letterforms inside the frame would be black and all those outside would be cream. The shapes around the letters became as important as the letters themselves, and by colouring them in randomly I reinforced the abstract quality of the overall design.

If you would like to attempt a lettering design, I recommend that you buy a thick marker pen and a pad of tracing paper. The pen will enable you to make big, bold letters and with the tracing paper you will be able to work on the design on different levels. For example, if you like part of what you have drawn, but not all of it, then you can overlay another sheet of paper to screen out the part you wish to ignore and concentrate on developing the area of the design you are happy with. A pad of tracing paper is a useful tool for building on your design by isolating elements that work, without the need to re-draw them.

I chose stranded cotton to stitch this project in order to give the work a lustrous quality and a crisp definition. The 16-gauge canvas provides plenty of detail and ensures smooth, straight lines of stitching.

opposite: Typography and lettering exist in thousands of different forms and provide the inspiration behind this Alphabet picture. (Christine Büttner)

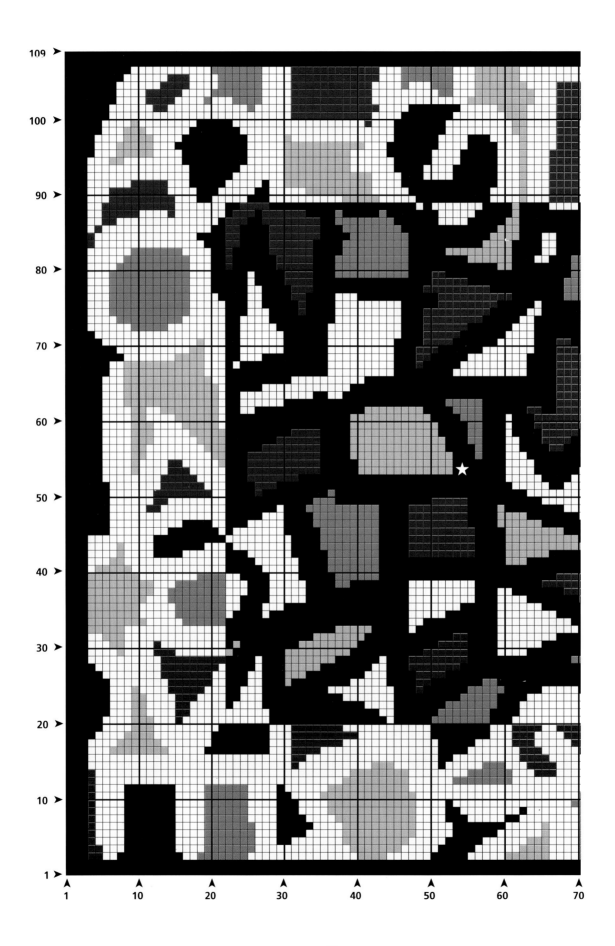

Use Anchor stranded cotton in the colours and quantities given in the key below. The initial numbers refer to the Anchor yarns; the numbers that follow in brackets refer to the number of skeins required. An 8 m (9 yd) skein will work approximately 1,152 stitches. (For DMC equivalents, see the conversion chart on page 140.)

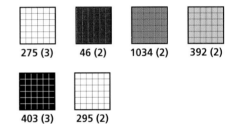

275 (3)   46 (2)   1034 (2)   392 (2)

403 (3)   295 (2)

☆ Mid-point of design

MATERIALS & EQUIPMENT

16-gauge canvas, 28 cm (11 in) square

Size 22 tapestry needle

Picture frame

The finished needlepoint measures 18 cm (7 in) square

Use all six strands of thread for stitching

CHINESE FIGURES

Chinese textiles, in particular embroideries, are among my main sources of inspiration. The Chinese have been weaving silk since about 4000 BC and by the 3rd century AD they were decorating clothing, wall hangings, furnishings and other textiles with embroidery. The art flourished over the following centuries and Chinese embroideries were highly prized and collected in Europe and North America, as they still are today.

Beautiful examples can be seen in the British Museum and the Victoria and Albert Museum, in London, in the Metropolitan Museum, in New York, and elsewhere. For instance, a set of stunning Chinese bed hangings that were made in the 18th century are on view to the public at Calke Abbey, a house in Derbyshire. The richly coloured silks and couched gold threads look like new as a result of the precious hangings being hidden in a trunk for the past 250 years!

Besides such grand, luxurious pieces, the Chinese have also produced many charming folk embroideries, which have a lively quality that I find especially appealing.

I decided to try to create a piece of needlepoint that would capture the same spirit that emanates from some of these embroideries. Many of them are gifts, often given at weddings, and because of this they convey happiness and good wishes. The characters that I chose for this needlepoint project symbolize good luck and longevity.

My first version of this ethnic needlepoint picture was worked on 18-gauge canvas in stranded cotton (see opposite) which is lustrous and so suggests the brilliance of the silk embroideries, in particular the rich, golden yellow that is so often used in Chinese art. I subsequently decided to make a larger version on 8-gauge canvas in double thickness tapestry wool to see the design with a matte finish. It is interesting to compare the two versions worked at a different scale and in different threads to see how the character of the piece changes.

You can take this approach one step further and change the colours in the needlepoint to produce an alternative colourway. For example, try using different colours for the clothing of the figures.

This design is much simpler to execute than it may at first appear. The easiest way to start is to work the top row and one of the side rows, using the yellow thread. Once you have positioned the work on the canvas you can stitch away as you please. When the work is finished and blocked (see page 136) take it to a professional framer and have it suitably mounted and framed.

opposite: The Chinese tradition of giving a piece of embroidery as a wedding present is a custom which you can continue today. (Caroline Robins)

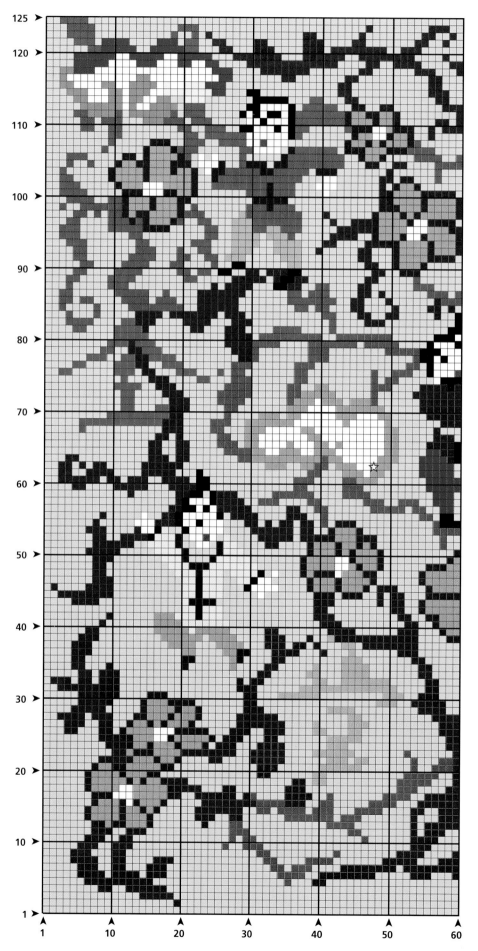

CHINESE PICTURE

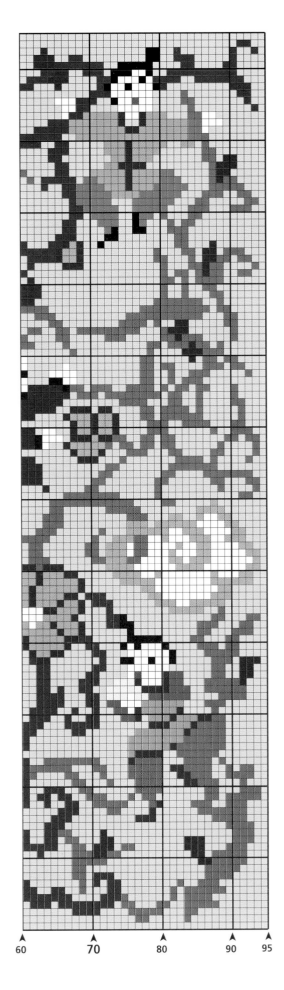

60   70   80   90   95

Use Anchor stranded cotton in the colours and quantities given in the key below. The initial numbers refer to the Anchor yarns; the numbers that follow in brackets refer to the number of skeins required. An 8 m (9 yd) skein will work approximately 1,450 stitches. (For DMC equivalents, see the conversion chart on page 140)

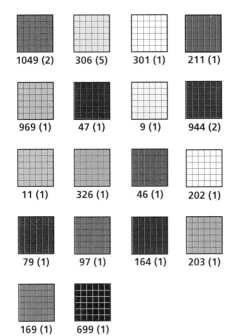

1049 (2)	306 (5)	301 (1)	211 (1)
969 (1)	47 (1)	9 (1)	944 (2)
11 (1)	326 (1)	46 (1)	202 (1)
79 (1)	97 (1)	164 (1)	203 (1)
169 (1)	699 (1)		

✧ Mid-point of design

MATERIALS & EQUIPMENT

18-gauge canvas, 28 x 23 cm (11 x 9 in)

Size 22 tapestry needle

Picture frame

The finished needlepoint measures 18 x 13.5 cm (7 x 5 ¼ in)

Use all six strands of threads for stitching

clothing

ANEMONE HAT

I made my anemone hat while living in Fontainebleau, in France, which was a happy and inspiring time. We were lucky enough to live in a delightful stone cottage on the edge of a forest which was full of glorious colours, especially in the autumn. One of the many pleasures of living there was cycling to the market. Sundays were most enjoyable and always began at our favourite café, sipping large cups of *café au lait* and eating fresh croissants. Then we would join the crowds in the marketplace. Whatever the time of year, the market was constantly full of shapes and colours to excite the senses and capture the imagination: mushrooms picked that morning in the forest, goat cheese brought by local farmers, and above all, flowers. The flower stalls were quite beautiful and I loved to take a bunch home with me to paint.

I had been sketching some anemones from the market when I came across an excellent hat design in a French craft magazine. I felt anemones would lend themselves well to needlepoint and that their sumptuous hues would make a gloriously colourful hat. A strong blue background seemed ideal to enhance the brightness of the petals.

Once I had completed my watercolour for the design in the required long, shallow rectangular shape, I drew the outline of the flowers on canvas. Then I filled in the areas using a luscious selection of yarns and watched the flowers take shape. The blossoms provided an opportunity to work with plenty of detail and tone.

To translate tone into needlepoint, first select a small area, perhaps a red petal. Now study your design carefully and look at your yarns. Select three shades of red – a light red for the palest, highlighted areas, a darker red for the areas in shadow and a medium red for the mid-tone. Then draw the outline of the petal on the canvas. If it helps, you can divide this area up into light, medium and dark areas, referring closely to your source material. After this careful preparation you can stitch the appropriate shades in the correct areas. For more subtle shading, break up the separate tonal areas by letting one encroach upon another. For example, add a random stitch of the dark shade at the edge of the medium area.

This design could be adapted in a variety of ways. You could make it as a narrower band of needlepoint, or use a larger-gauge canvas to complete the work more quickly. You could even use the basic elongated rectangular shape as a starting point for your own original design, perhaps adapting a floral motif from a different source.

opposite: The rich colours of anemones translate beautifully onto canvas. This design developed out of a bunch of anemones I bought at a French market. (Caroline Robins)

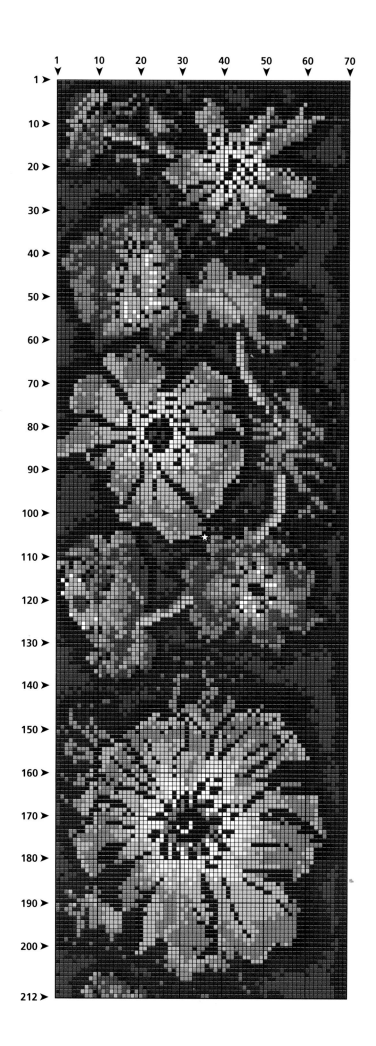

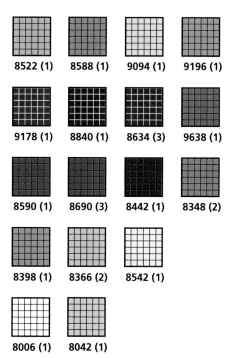

Use Anchor wool in the colours and quantities given in the key below. The initial numbers refer to the Anchor yarns; the numbers that follow in brackets refer to the number of skeins required. A 10 m (11 yd) skein will work at least 1,200 stitches. (For DMC equivalents see the conversion chart on page 141.)

8522 (1)	8588 (1)	9094 (1)	9196 (1)
9178 (1)	8840 (1)	8634 (3)	9638 (1)
8590 (1)	8690 (3)	8442 (1)	8348 (2)
8398 (1)	8366 (2)	8542 (1)	
8006 (1)	8042 (1)		

☆ Mid-point of design

A section of the chart must be repeated in mirror image to complete the design. Begin stitching at row 212, placing this about 5 cm (2 in) from the left-hand edge of the canvas. When you reach row 1 repeat the design, working from row 81 back to row 1.

ANEMONE HAT

MATERIALS & EQUIPMENT

15-gauge canvas, 22 x 68 cm (9 x 27 in)

Felt, at least 20 cm (8 in) square

20 cm (¼ yd) of lining fabric

60 cm (¾ yd) of narrow braid

60 cm (¾ yd) of 3 cm (1¼ in) wide velvet ribbon

Strong dark blue sewing thread

Size 18 tapestry needle

Compass

Measures 58 cm (23 in) in circumference and 13 cm (4¾ in) in depth

Use one strand of yarn for stitching

Determining the size

1 The chart shown is for a hat 58 cm (23 in) in circumference. Measure your head to see if this size will suit you. To make the hat a different size, note this measurement and alter the chart accordingly; note that there are 16 threads to 1 in (or 6.3 to 1 cm).

2 Once you know the circumference, calculate the size of the crown, with the formula: circumference divided by π (3.1416). This gives the diameter of the circle. Divide by two for the radius. Set the compass to this measurement and draw a circle onto paper to use as a pattern for the top. If you are making a hat of the same size as the one shown, set the radius at 9.2 cm (3⅝ in).

Making up instructions

1 Block the needlepoint (see page 136). Trim the canvas to 4 cm (1½ in) all around.

2 From the felt, cut out a circle for the top of the hat, using the pattern already drawn.

From the lining fabric cut out a rectangle 14 x 60 cm (5½ x 23½ in). Cut out a circle of lining fabric, using the pattern and add 1 cm (⅜ in) seam allowance all around.

3 Fold under the unworked canvas on the short ends of the needlepoint and baste it in place. Close the edges together with tiny oversewing stitches (see Techniques, page 138) and stitch with the dark blue thread (a).

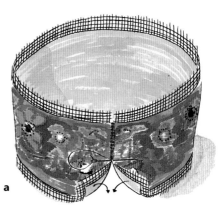
a

4 Turn under and baste the unworked canvas on the top edge. Sew the circle of felt to this edge, using matching thread and tiny oversewing stitches (b). Leave a small gap in this seam near the other (side) seam.

5 Pin the braid around the top edge of the hat, covering the top seam and slipstitch it in place (see Techniques, page 138). Trim the ends of the braid to 2 cm (1 in) and tuck them into the gap, so they cross each other smoothly. Hand stitch them in place and close the gap around them.

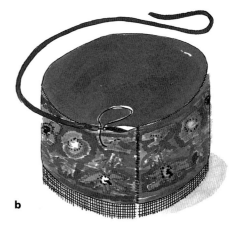
b

6 Join the short ends of the rectangular lining piece with a 1.5 cm (⅝ in) seam. Press the seam open. Pin, baste and stitch the circular piece to the edge, taking a 1 cm (⅜ in) seam. With the lining still turned wrong side out, insert it into the hat. Make sure it fits snugly, then baste it to the inside of the hat, just above the edge of the needlepoint (c). Trim the raw edge so that it extends below the needlepoint by 1 cm (⅜ in).

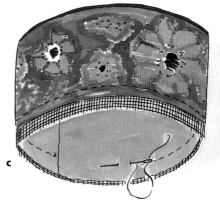
c

7 Trim the lower edge of the canvas so that it is even with the lining. Slipstitch one edge of the ribbon to the front of the needlepoint (see page 138). Then fold the ribbon to the wrong side, covering the canvas edges and sew it in place (d). Overlap the ends neatly, turning under the top end.

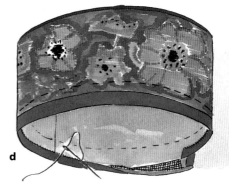
d

MASK

While we were living in France, we received an invitation to a masked ball, which was to be held in a château near Paris. Here was an exciting opportunity to apply my needlepoint to making something glamorous and frivolous – a chance not to be missed!

Although most of us are accustomed to seeing traditional needlepoint objects such as cushions, chair seats, stool tops and evening bags, there is no reason to restrict the craft to such projects. Needlepoint is very versatile, and along with giving the designs themselves a contemporary look, we should also explore new ways of using it.

A masked ball is not a common event these days, but there are other occasions when a mask is appropriate, such as a fancy dress party. For children, the Hallowe'en "trick or treat" custom requires disguising the face by wearing a mask. And when the party's over, the mask can make a striking decoration on a dressing table or hung on a wall. One which is worked in needlepoint is sure to attract attention.

The mask should, of course, coordinate with the rest of the outfit. The one shown here, with its subtle-coloured streamers of gray-blue, white and pale gold against a black background, I designed for my husband to match a black tie and dinner jacket.

For the same evening I created a different, more flamboyant design in brilliant red and green for myself and a third for a friend showing a motif of shooting stars. The ball was a magnificent occasion and I still carry vivid memories of candlelit rooms, champagne, and people dancing and parading with a dazzling array of masks.

If you wish to design your own mask you have all sorts of options. Printed fabrics often contain motifs that can be adapted for the purpose. Make sure that you choose something that harmonizes with what you intend to wear. Alternatively, you could use one of the designs, or part of a design from any other project in this book.

To make a mask of your own design, draw the outline of the chart shown overleaf onto graph paper and alter the design as you wish. Note that your chart may be smaller or larger than the mask, depending on the scale of the graph paper and your choice of canvas; you should check your measurements to ensure that the mask will fit the wearer before you begin filling in the design. By following the chart you can make a mask to fit an adult with an average-size head. If you wish to make minor adjustments, such as altering the size of the eye holes; make the alterations before you begin stitching.

opposite: Make your own mask for a dramatic addition to a costume for a fancy-dress party or Hallowe'en. (Caroline Robins)

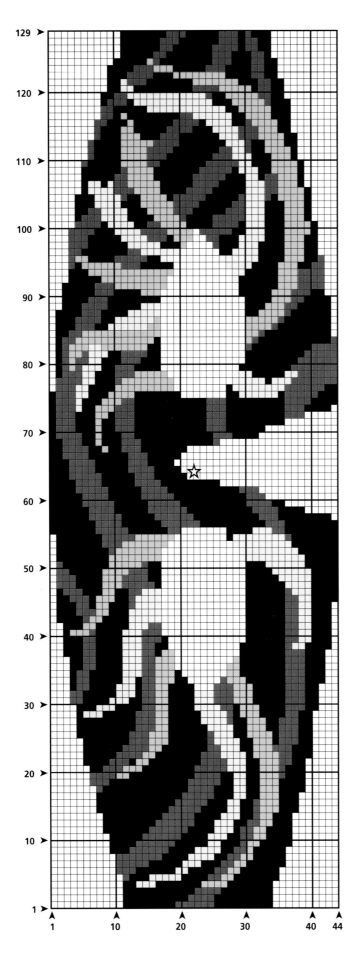

Use Anchor tapestry wool in the colours and quantities given in the key below. The initial numbers refer to the Anchor yarns; the numbers that follow in brackets refer to the number of skeins required. A 10 m (11 yd) skein will work approximately 1,200 stitches. (For DMC equivalents, see the conversion chart on page 141.)

| 9800 (2) | 8736 (2) | 8018 (1) | 8032 (1) |

☆ Mid-point of design

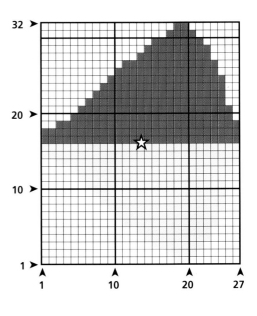

MASK

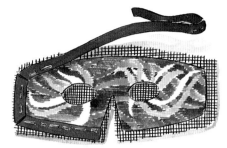

a

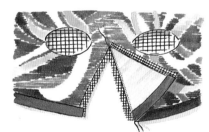

b

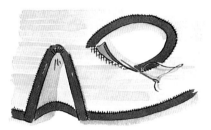

c

d

e

MATERIALS & EQUIPMENT

14-gauge canvas, 20 x 45 cm (8 x 18 in)

1.2 m (1¼ yd) of 3 cm (1¼ in) wide bias

binding; or about 20 cm (¼ yd) of fabric

for making binding

50 cm (½ yd) of 5 mm (¼ in) wide elastic

1 m (1 yd) of 2.5 cm (1 in) wide ribbon

Size 18 tapestry needle

Measures 10 x 26 cm (4 x 10½ in)

Use one strand of yarn for stitching

Making up instructions

1 First block or stretch the needlepoint. If you cannot have this done professionally, then follow the instructions given in the Techniques section on page 136. Trim the canvas to 1 cm (⅜ in) along the outer edges.

2 If you are making your own binding, cut out 3 cm (1¼ in) wide strips, as described on page 138. Join them up to make a length of at least 112 cm (44 in).

3 Starting on the lower edge of the mask, just beside the nose opening, pin the binding along the edges of the needlepoint, with right sides facing and the edges matching. Baste as you go and gather the binding slightly at the corners, so that it will be full enough to go over the edge of the canvas (a). (This can be trimmed later if necessary.) Continue to the other side of the nose; cut off the excess binding. Machine stitch the binding in place, working just inside the edge of the needlepoint to prevent any bare canvas from showing. If you do not have access to a sewing machine, use backstitch (see page 137).

4 Fold the binding over the edge of the canvas. Turn under the raw edge (b) and slipstitch it to the wrong side of the needlepoint (see Techniques, page 138).

5 Apply another strip of binding to the lower edge of the nose, following the instructions described in steps 3 and 4.

6 Pin the nose and the main piece together with right sides facing and two of the canvas edges aligned (c). Baste and machine stitch. Repeat to join the remaining edges.

7 Cover the raw edges of the canvas around the nose with binding, turning under the binding edges and slipstitch them firmly in place. Trim the canvas a little if required for a more comfortable fit.

8 Cut out the eye holes, leaving about 5 mm (¼ in) of canvas all around. Starting at the inner corner of each eye, pin, baste and machine stitch binding around the edge, as described in step 3. Trim the binding as required to fit these narrower canvas edges, then slipstitch it (d) to the wrong side of the eye hole (see page 138).

9 Sew one end of the elastic neatly and securely with hand stitches to one upper corner of the mask. Try the mask on, and pin the elastic to the other corner. Trim off the excess and sew the other end of the elastic firmly in place.

10 Cut the length of ribbon in two. Fold under one end of each length in order to neaten it, and sew this to the edge of the mask over the elastic. Trim the ends to form a "V" shape, as shown in the illustration (e). When wearing the mask, tie the ribbons over the elastic at the back of the head in order to conceal it.

BOW-TIE

When I saw the stills from Christine's film relating colour and music (see the Starburst spectacles case on page 109), I was immediately inspired to use one of them for a project of my own. The vibrant colours were irresistible and the abstract shapes lent themselves well to an accessory such as a bow tie. From the outset, I envisaged this as a tie for a boy; something to wear on a festive occasion, such as a birthday party or a family celebration. But it really is as suitable for the young at heart as well as for the young in years. Because it is a false tie, attached to elastic to slip over the head, it will appeal to those who find tying the genuine article a vexing task. Indeed, the speed with which this small-scale project can be stitched makes it equally appealing to the stitcher!

You could adapt the basic idea by using whatever pattern you like. A simple spattering of dots would work well, or perhaps a fragment of tartan, as the fine canvas permits a fair amount of detail. A diagonal stripe or a lozenge pattern could also be effective. However, consider that when the tie is completed it will be scrunched slightly in the middle, so it is best to avoid a highly representational design which would become distorted. There are all sorts of places you can turn to for design ideas. For instance,

take a look at photographs or postcards of paintings which can often yield interesting abstract shapes, especially if you zoom in on a small area. To attempt this, cut out two "L" shapes from stiff paper or card. Place them over your chosen image so that they form a rectangular "window". This technique is used by graphic designers to bring a specific area of an image into focus. By moving the position of the two "L" shapes you can adjust the size and shape of the window until you find part of the image that appeals to you. Next, tape or place a weight on the "L" shapes to hold them in place and then trace off the image inside the window. You can alter the size of the design by enlarging it on a photocopier, or by scaling up the image using the method described on page 139. Keep the original source to hand as a guide for the colours. Or, you may wish to change the colours; an interesting exercise is to make a black and white photocopy of the original material which will show up the tonal values without the distraction of the actual hues. You can then interpret the design with whatever colours you desire.

I chose a rich, royal blue silk to line my bow tie to enhance the festive look. Any type of fabric that is easy to handle, such as silk or a soft cotton, is suitable for lining.

opposite: A vibrant bow tie will provide a splash of colour against formal evening wear, or lend a touch of character on any occasion. (Caroline Robins)

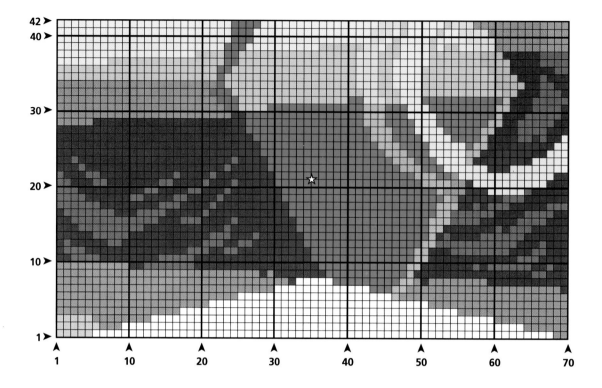

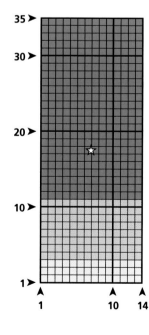

Use Anchor stranded cotton in the colours and quantities given in the key below. The initial numbers refer to the Anchor yarns; the numbers that follow in brackets refer to the number of skeins required. An 8 m (9 yd) skein will work approximately 1,456 stitches. (For DMC equivalents, see the conversion chart on page 140.)

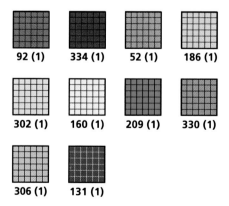

92 (1) 334 (1) 52 (1) 186 (1)

302 (1) 160 (1) 209 (1) 330 (1)

306 (1) 131 (1)

☆ **Mid-point of design**

MATERIALS & EQUIPMENT

18-gauge canvas, 10 x 27 cm (4 x 10½ in)

Silk or cotton fabric, 8 x 12 cm (3 x 5 in)

50 cm (½ yd) of cord elastic

Size 20 tapestry needle

Measures 6 x 10 cm (2¼ x 4 in)

Use all six strands of the thread for stitching. Work the main piece and the rectangular strip on one piece of canvas, allowing 5 cm (2 in) between them

Making up instructions

1 First block or stretch the needlepoint. If you cannot have this done professionally, follow the instructions on page 136. Trim the canvas on both pieces to 1 cm (⅜ in).

2 On the small rectangle cut away the excess canvas at the corners in order to reduce the bulk (a). Turn under the top and bottom edges and press, then turn under the side edges, taking in the edge of the needlepoint to prevent any bare canvas from showing. Press, then oversew (see page 138) the canvas edges together, at the same time catching in the wrong side of the needlepoint (a).

3 Pin and baste the main piece of the needlepoint to the lining fabric, with right sides facing. Machine stitch along the side and lower edges, just inside the stitched area, in order to prevent any bare canvas from showing (b). If you do not have access to a sewing machine, use backstitch instead (see page 137). Trim the canvas edges to about 5 mm (¼ in) and trim off the sharp corners diagonally.

4 Turn the bow right side out. Turn in the canvas and fabric edges along the top (c). Slipstitch them together (see page 138).

5 Form the elastic into a ring to fit the required neck measurement comfortably, without stretching, and knot the ends together. Double-check the measurement. Trim off the excess elastic. Hand sew the knot neatly and securely to the wrong side of one end of the strip (d).

6 Make a couple of folds in the bow tie, and fit the strip around the middle, butting the ends together. Sew the ends together (e).

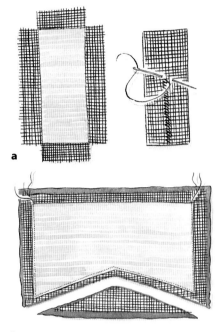

a

b

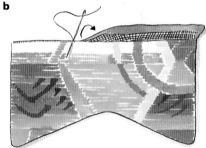

c

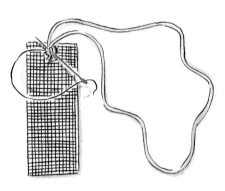

d

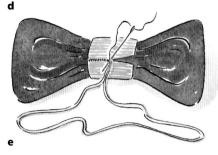

e

BLOOMSBURY WAISTCOAT

This waistcoat is one of my most ambitious projects to date. It took me a long time to settle on a subject for it – I considered all manner of images, including plaids, figures, flora and fauna. Eventually I decided on a design inspired by the Bloomsbury group. This was a group of friends who, in the early 1900s, used to gather together at the home of the painter Vanessa Bell in Bloomsbury, a part of London, to exchange ideas on a wide range of subjects. Out of these discussions developed a certain style and approach to art and craft, and, in a much broader sense, to life itself. In 1910 the art critic Roger Fry, a member of the group, organized the first Post-Impressionist exhibition in London. For the Bloomsbury group the works by Van Gogh, Gauguin, Picasso, Matisse and Cézanne were an inspiration, but the art establishment branded them as crude and immoral. In 1913 Fry founded the Omega Workshops. Here, young artists and craftsmen began to apply some of the ideas and theories of the Post-Impressionists to three-dimensional designs. The range of items produced through Omega was enormous and touched many areas: rugs, fabrics, screens, murals, book illustration, clothes, tiles and interiors; the artists were prepared to tackle almost any medium.

In 1916 Vanessa Bell discovered Charleston. It was then a ramshackle Sussex farmhouse, but it was to become the embodiment of a way of art and life and a home to the group. The work produced at Charleston has an exuberant, free style. It is unrestrained and spills through the house: walls, doors, window frames, chairs, floors – not a surface has been left untouched. In among the paintings and furniture there are pieces of needlepoint: cushions, fire screens, hangings and upholstery, all executed with the same joyful feeling and with a wonderful use of colour.

To the best of my knowledge there isn't actually a waistcoat in the Charleston museum, but I like to think that there might have been and that the group would have approved of the idea. The waistcoat was inspired by a stitched fire screen designed by Duncan Grant. I like the idea of working on an asymmetrical design, creating something which is a little quirky and unexpected. Having composed the complete image for the left front of the waistcoat, I took the individual elements and spilled them over the opposite shoulder as though they were tumbling into place. Waistcoats are useful items to have in any wardrobe; they can be worn with formal dress or quite casually with jeans and a shirt.

opposite: My most ambitious project to date is a waistcoat. The asymmetrical pattern was inspired by a stitched fire screen designed by Duncan Grant. (Christine Büttner)

Use Anchor wool in the colours and quantities given in the key on the right. The initial numbers refer to the Anchor yarns; the numbers that follow in brackets refer to the number of skeins required. A 10 m (11 yd) skein will work approximately 950 stitches. (For DMC equivalents, see the conversion chart on page 141.)

9768 (16)   9052 (1)   9016 (1)   8834 (1)

☆ **Mid-point of design**

8544 (2)   8504 (1)   8038 (3)

8216 (2)   8034 (1)

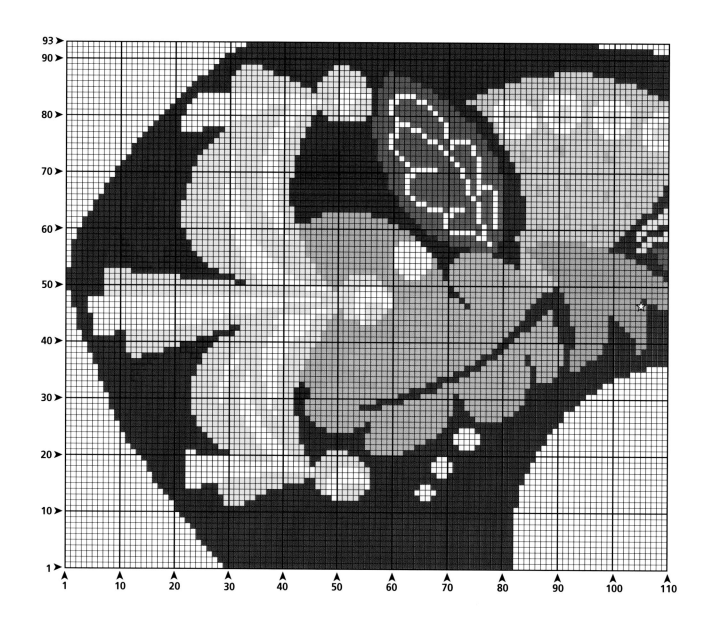

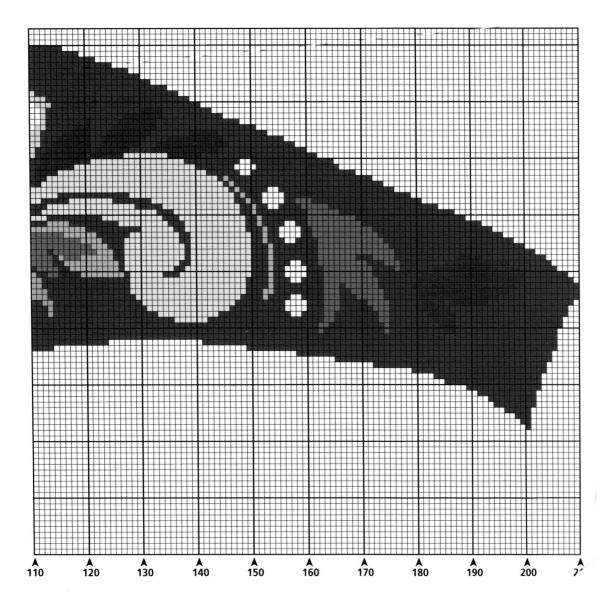

110   120   130   140   150   160   170   180   190   200   2

Use Anchor wool in the colours and quantities given in the key on the right. The initial numbers refer to the Anchor yarns; the numbers that follow in brackets refer to the number of skeins required. A 10 m (11 yd) skein will work approximately 950 stitches. (For DMC equivalents, see the conversion chart on page 141.)

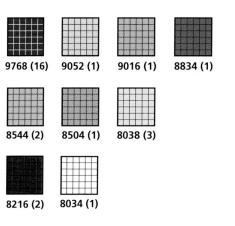

9768 (16) 9052 (1) 9016 (1) 8834 (1)

8544 (2) 8504 (1) 8038 (3)

8216 (2) 8034 (1)

☆ Mid-point of design

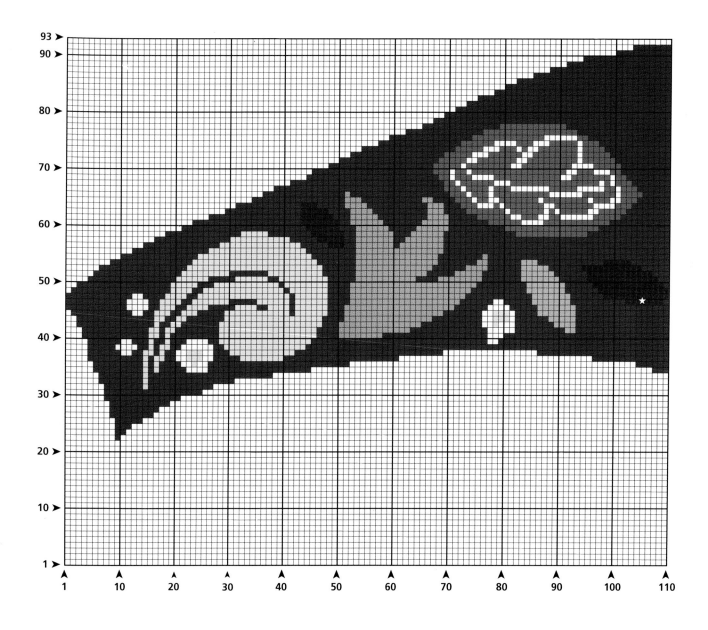

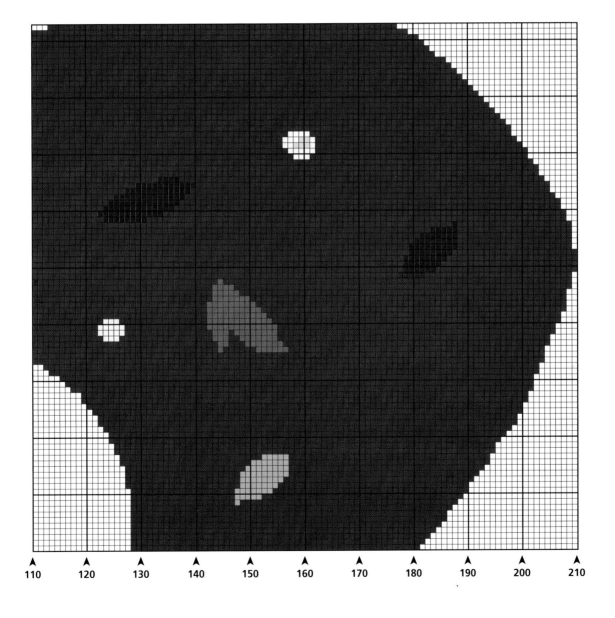

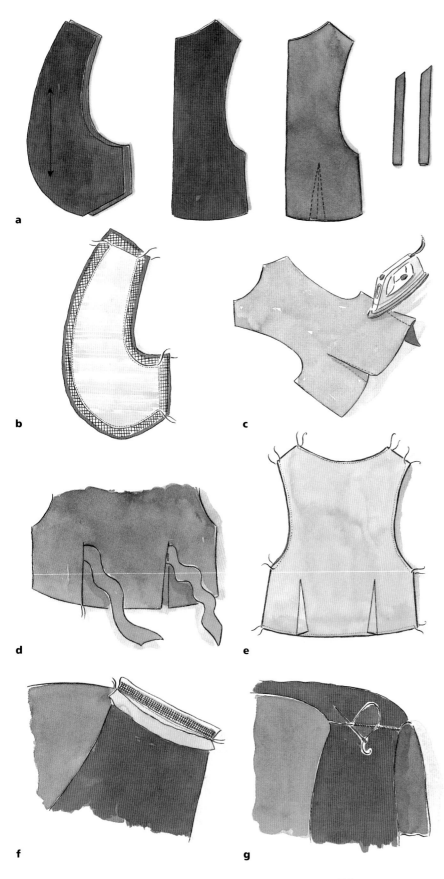

a

b

c

d

e

f

g

MATERIALS & EQUIPMENT

10-gauge canvas, 62 x 70 cm (24 x 27 in)

60 cm (⅝ yd) of medium-weight linen, or other fabric, for the back and ties

60 cm (⅝ yd) of lining fabric

Strong sewing thread

Size 18 tapestry needle

Two sheets of graph paper, at least 54 x 28 cm (21½ x 11 in)

Tracing wheel and dressmaker's carbon paper (optional)

Measures approximately 88 cm (34¼ in) in width

Use one strand of thread for stitching

Making up instructions

1 First block or stretch the finished pieces of needlepoint. I strongly recommend that you have this done by a professional. However, if you choose to do the blocking yourself, follow the instructions in the Techniques section on page 136. Trim the canvas edges to 1.5 cm (⅝ in) all around.

2 To make the patterns for the front, back and ties of the waistcoat, enlarge the outlines (a) given according to the specified size that you require with the aid of graph paper (follow the instructions for scaling designs up and down in the Techniques section on page 139). Use these patterns to cut out the required pieces from the main fabric and the lining, as shown in the diagram (a). I chose to use a charcoal-gray linen for the main fabric and a scarlet silk for the lining, both fabrics complement the colours in the needlepoint design. (If the lining has a right and a wrong side, remember to reverse the pattern for one piece.) Using either tailor's tacks or dressmaker's carbon paper and a tracing wheel, transfer the dart markings onto the fabric.

As an alternative to drawing up your own pattern, you may find it simpler to purchase a waistcoat pattern and follow the manufacturer's instructions. If you choose this option then you will have to make sure that your finished needlepoint is the required size for the front left- and right-hand side of the wasitcoat pattern.

3 On each piece of needlepoint, turn the front/lower and armhole edges to the wrong side and press with the point of an iron, including 3 mm (⅛ in) of the needle-

point. This pre-pressing will help to achieve crisp edges. Now place one lining front and one needlepoint front together with right sides facing and the raw edges matching. Pin and baste the two pieces together. Note that the lining is slightly smaller than the needlepoint. Machine stitch the two layers together, just inside the edge of the needlepoint, leaving the side and shoulder edges open (b). Repeat on the other front section of the waistcoat. If you do not have access to a sewing machine then use a neat, firm backstitch instead, see the Techniques section on page 137. However, note that backstitch will not be as strong as sewing by machine.

4 Trim away the edges of the canvas and lining to approximately 3 mm (⅛ in). With the points of a sharp pair of scissors, clip the curved edges if necessary, so that the fabric lies flat. Turn the left- and right-hand fronts right side out. Use a knitting needle or a similar object to turn the seams out fully. Baste around the edges to flatten them, then press them carefully with the point of an iron before you remove the basting stitches.

5 To make the ties for the back of the waistcoat (see the photograph on page 68), fold each one in half lengthways, right sides together. Pin and neatly stitch close to the long and diagonal edges. Trim the seam allowances to 5 mm (¼ in). Turn the ties right side out, using a knitting needle. Press with the point of an iron. If you wish, you can strengthen the tie with decorative topstitch 3 mm (⅛ in) from the edges, see the Techniques section, page 138.

6 On the main back piece, press the middle line of each dart to the wrong side (c). Insert the unfinished end of each tie into the fold. Make sure that the point is turned upward on the left tie and downward on the right tie; this will produce a neat bow, with both ties pointing downward. Pin the ties in place. Baste, then stitch the darts, catching one tie in each dart at the same time (d). Press the darts in toward the middle using the point of an iron.

7 Pin, baste and stitch the darts in the back lining piece.

8 Place the two back pieces – the main fabric and the lining – together with right sides facing and the raw edges matching. (Note that here too the lining is slightly smaller than the outer piece.) Pin and baste along the armhole, neck and lower edges. Machine stitch 1.5 cm (⅝ in) from the edge (e). Trim the seam to 5 mm (¼ in), clip the curves with the points of a pair of sharp scissors to help the fabric lie flat and turn the work right side out through one of the side openings. Press the stitched edges carefully, pushing the main fabric to the inside.

9 Pin the back and one front section together at the shoulder. Baste and stitch the main fabric and the edges of the needlepoint together (f). Trim the seam allowances to 5 mm (¼ in) and press the seams open. Repeat to join the other front at the shoulder. Turn under the edges of the lining on the front and back shoulder and slipstitch (g) them together (see Techniques, page 138).

10 Repeat the previous step to join the back to the fronts at the side edges.

FISH HAT

The inspiration behind this project was an elegant linen skirt that I had treated myself to, purchased from my favourite designers, Workers for Freedom. The skirt is brown with deep navy floral motifs scattered across it. I hadn't previously thought of brown and navy as a particularly interesting combination, and yet here it worked successfully.

Using the skirt as a starting point, I began by making some rough scribbles, in order to gauge the effect of different tones and shades. The next step was to play with the yarns themselves. This is perhaps the most exciting stage of the design process, when you begin to see all the colours reacting together. I decided that an almost blue-black worked well with a substantially lighter brown and then I turned my thoughts to how to add some zest to these rather mute colours, while still wishing to keep the work to a restricted palette. The ultimate challenge in creating your own design is to achieve a balance among the final selection of colours. After many trials which involved holding various skeins of threads together, I settled on three additional colours: turquoise – a frivolous and lively relative of the blue-black, a bright orange – a flamboyant associate of the brown, and to really liven things up, a brilliant, pure primary yellow.

I wanted the shapes in the design to have the kind of spontaneous feel of paper cut-outs and so I actually took scissors to paper to get the real sense of how these shapes should be formed. I then experimented with positioning the various cut-outs and layering them. When eventually I was happy with the way the cut-outs related to each other, I traced them onto tracing paper and transferred the design onto the canvas.

I knew from the start that the stitched panel was going to form the decorative panel on a hat, but I did waver between whether or not it should have a brim. In the end I must admit that it came down to practicalities; because of the difficulty of making a flat brim, I settled for a pillbox shape, with the needlepoint forming an outer layer, to give the effect of an upturned brim. To liven the whole thing up I added a pair of long ties at the back. I am particularly fond of bows and ribbons as a means of fastening; apart from their obvious decorative quality, as compared to zips or hooks, they are also much easier to attach.

If you don't find my choice of colours suitable for your wardrobe, then feel free to make up your own palette. Any five colours will achieve the same sort of balance, but you could add more hues for a busier effect.

opposite: The famous cut-outs by Henri Matisse and the colours in a favourite skirt prompted this Fish hat. You can alter the colours in the design to suit your wardrobe. (Christine Büttner)

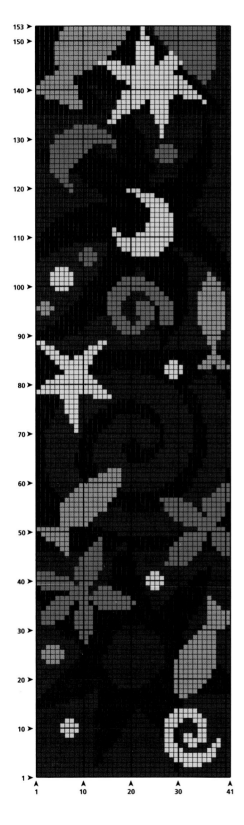

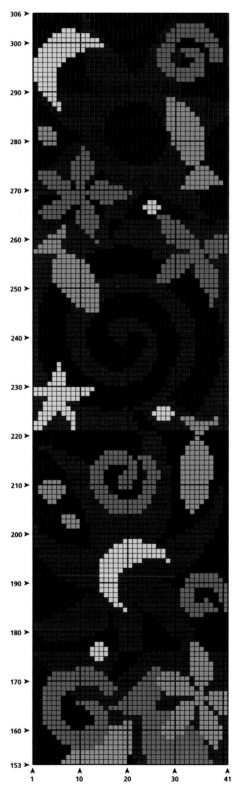

Use Anchor tapestry wool in the colours and quantities given in the key below. The initial numbers refer to the Anchor codes; the numbers that follow in brackets refer to the number of skeins required. A 10 m (11 yd) skein will work approximately 1,040 stitches. (For DMC equivalents, see the conversion chart on page 141.)

8744 (4)   8168 (1)   8122 (1)

9644 (6)   8808 (2)

MATERIALS & EQUIPMENT

13-gauge canvas, 18 x 68 cm (7 x 27 in)
Fabric for lining needlepoint, size of finished stitched area plus 1.5 cm (⅝ in) seam allowances
20 cm (¼ yd) velvet for crown
20 cm (¼ yd) calico or cotton
Strong sewing thread
Compass
Size 20 tapestry needle

Measures approximately 8 cm (3 in) in depth and 58 cm (23 in) in circumference
Use one strand of yarn for stitching

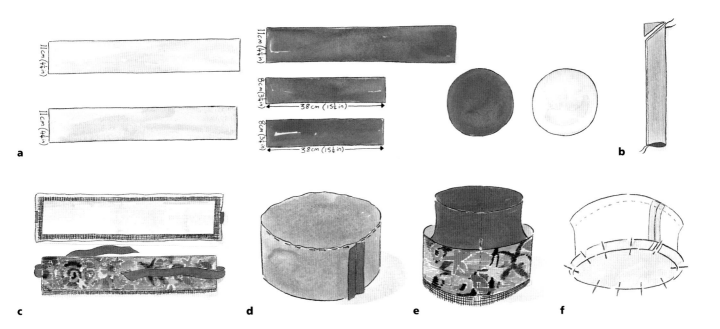

a

b

c   d   e   f

Determining the size

The chart opposite is for a hat that is 58 cm (23 in) in circumference. For a different size, note this measurement and alter the chart accordingly. There are 13 threads to 1 in (five to 1 cm). To calculate the size of the top of the crown, see step 2, on page 59. For this hat, the radius is 10.7 cm (4¼ in).

Making up instructions

1 Block the needlepoint (see page 136). Trim the canvas to 1 cm (⅜ in) along the top and sides and to 2 cm (¾ in) at the bottom.

2 Cut out the pieces of velvet from the pattern already drawn (a); a rectangle 11 cm (4¼ in) by the required length plus 3 cm (1¼ in) and two strips for the ties, 38 cm x 8 cm (15¼ x 3¼ in). From the calico cut a circle and a rectangle the same sizes as for the velvet.

3 Make the ties. Fold each strip in half lengthways, right sides together. Machine stitch close to the long cut edges, ending 3.5 cm (1½ in) from the end. Pivot the work

45° and stitch to the end. Tie the thread ends. Trim the excess fabric at the point (b). Turn the strip right side out. Press the strips, then topstitch close to the edges.

4 Place the needlepoint lining right side up. Position and pin the ties on top, with the short open ends aligned with the side edges of lining, 2.5 cm (1 in) from the top.

5 Lay the needlepoint right side down on the lining and ties, the deeper canvas seam allowance at the bottom. Pin and baste together. Machine stitch around the side and top edges, just within the stitched area (c). Trim the corners at a 45° angle.

6 Turn the work right side out. Press. Pin the open edges together. Topstitch 5 mm (¼ in) from the edge around the side and top edges, then across the open edges.

7 Join the short ends of the velvet rectangle, right sides facing, and stitch, taking 1.5 cm (⅝ in) seam allowance. Pin the circular top piece to one edge of the cylindrical section right sides facing (d). Baste and

stitch. Turn the piece right side out. Repeat to assemble the lining for the crown. Leave the lining wrong side out and lay it aside.

8 Fold the needlepoint in half and mark the mid point with a pin. Mark the middle front of the velvet crown, opposite the seam with a pin. Place the needlepoint, right side out, over the velvet crown, aligning the markers. Pin the edges together all around (e). The previously worked seam (see step 6) should lie 1.5 cm (⅝ in) above the raw edge of the velvet. Baste, then machine stitch over the first line of stitching.

9 Trim away the excess velvet and lining fabric. Fold the canvas edges up into the inside of the hat and baste in place.

10 Fit the lining (f) into the hat. Turn under the lower edge and pin the hem in place, through the lining. Remove the lining. Press the folded edge and remove the pins. Replace the lining in the hat. Pin and baste the edges. Slipstitch the edges together (see page 138). Tie the ties into a bow.

TARTAN CUMMERBUND

Having completed my tartan cushion (see page 31) and realized how well tartan lends itself to needlepoint, I was eager to experiment further with plaids and checks and I wanted to attempt to combine several different tartans within one project. In the meantime I had bought myself a cummerbund. It was made of wool with a rich paisley pattern and I was delighted with the way it could instantly transform a somewhat dull dress into an eye-catching outfit. The two ideas seemed to merge and so I found myself planning a tartan cummerbund.

Even though I was already familiar with many tartans, I was amazed to find such a variety of designs and colours used for them. Some of the combinations are quite audacious, and by-passing some of the more restrained examples, I succumbed to the vibrant pinks in the McNab tartan, the hot yellow of MacPherson and the rich purples of the MacLeod of Lewis, which I thought would work well together. The MacLeod and the MacPherson alternate across the front of the cummerbund, with the McNab providing a little extra excitement at the back, see the charts overleaf. The back section of tartan (not visible in the photograph) is worked on a slightly finer-gauge canvas than the other two to allow for greater detail.

For lining the cummerbund, my remnant box yielded a soft, dark blue wool, which was easy to handle and lovely to work with. You could choose any of the tartan colours to line your own cummerbund. For the fastening at the front a length of thin yellow velvet ribbon, chosen to match the MacPherson yellow, seemed appropriate. This lacing not only looks attractive but it also makes the cummerbund accommodate a range of waist sizes. As a final embellishment I added a kilt pin.

You can start by making any of the sections of the cummerbund. Once you have worked a small part of the pattern, it is a good idea to work some of the major grid lines from top to bottom and from side to side. This will serve as a framework to help you keep the pattern correct. The tapestry wool works very well on the finer canvas. On the coarser canvas you will find it necessary to work with a fairly loose tension in order to get good coverage.

If you are an inexperienced dressmaker, the five separate piece of needlepoint may look somewhat daunting, but don't be put off. This garment really is not difficult to make. Do not worry if you stray slightly from the chart and be prepared to sacrifice a few rows of needlepoint for a good fit.

opposite: Spurred on by my tartan cushion (see page 31) I incorporated three tartans – the McNab, the MacLeod of Lewis and the MacPherson into this cummerbund. (Caroline Robins)

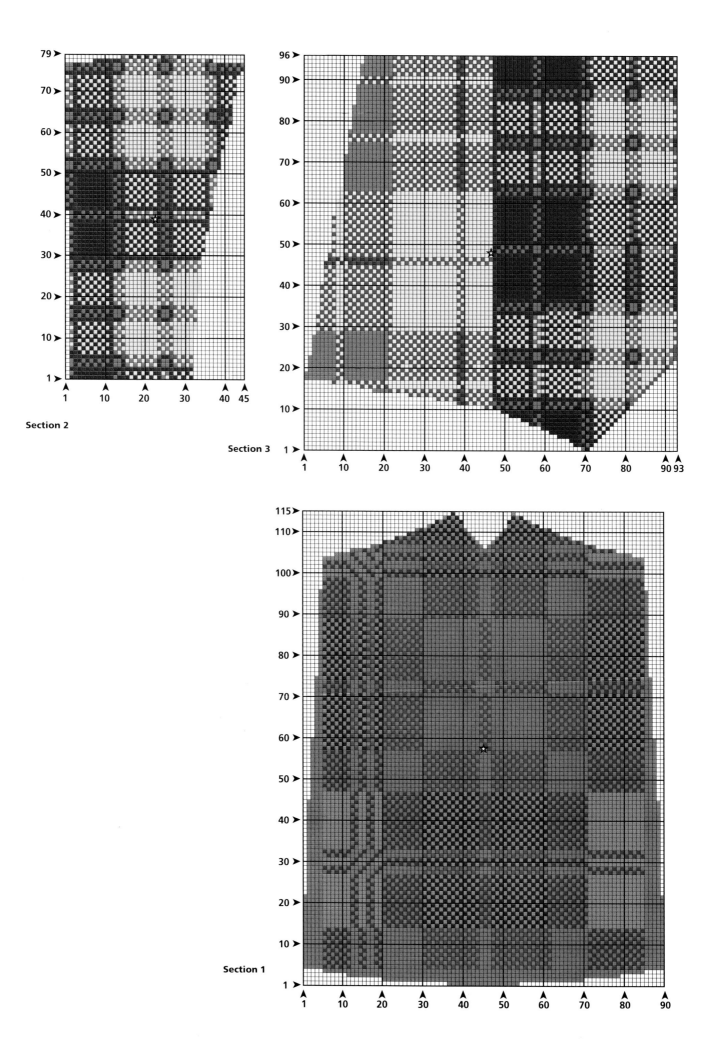

Section 2

Section 3

Section 1

TARTAN CUMMERBUND

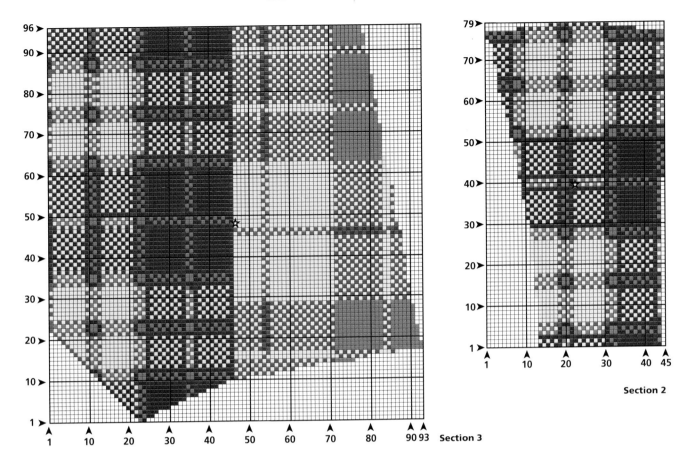

Section 2

Section 3

Use Anchor tapestry wool in the colours and quantities given in the key on the right. The initial numbers refer to the Anchor codes; the numbers that follow in brackets refer to the number of skeins required. A 10m (11 yd) skein will work approximately 950/1200 stitches. (For DMC equivalents, see the conversion chart on page 141.)

8986 (2) 9078 (1) 9766 (1) 8264 (1)

8454 (3) 8200 (3) 9052 (8) 8608 (3)

8118 (5) 9764 (1) 8198 (2) 8596 (8)

☆ Mid-point of design

Section 1 = McNab

Section 2 = MacLeod

Section 3 = MacLeod and MacPherson

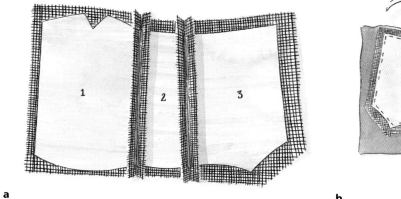

a

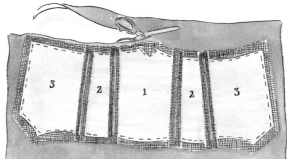

b

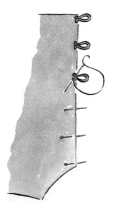

c

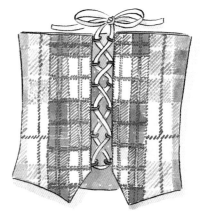

d

MATERIALS & EQUIPMENT

10-gauge canvas, 35 x 90 cm (14 x 35 in)

13-gauge canvas, 32 x 28 cm (13 x 11 in)

30 cm (⅜ yd) of lightweight wool, or

other fabric suitable for the lining

2 m (2¼ yd) of narrow velvet ribbon for

lacing the cummerbund together

A dozen large, curved eyes suitable for

use on coats

Strong sewing thread in matching

colours

Size 18 tapestry needle

Measures approximately 67 cm (26½ in)

along the top edge

Use one strand of thread for stitching on

10-gauge canvas for the MacPherson and

MacLeod tartans, and 13-gauge canvas for

the McNab tartan

Sections 1, 2 and 3 can be worked on sep-

arate pieces of canvas, or all together on

one uncut piece

Making up instructions

1 First block or stretch the finished piece (or pieces) of needlepoint. I strongly recommended that you have this done by a professional. However, if you choose to do the blocking yourself at home, follow the instructions in the Techniques section on page 136. If you have stitched the needlepoint on separate pieces of canvas then you should *individually* block or stretch each section. Trim off the edges of the canvas to 1.5 cm (⅝ in) all around.

2 Pin one section 2 to section 1 (as shown in illustration a, opposite) placing the right sides together and taking care to position the narrower edge of 2 on the top, so that it aligns with the notched edge of 1. Baste the two sections together along the two adjoining sides, using a double strand of strong sewing thread. (A single strand is much more liable to break.) Then join one section 3 to section 2 (as shown in illustration a, opposite) along the yellow tartan edge on the two adjoining sides. Baste the remaining sections 2 and 3 to the other side of section 1 (as shown in illustration b, opposite) to form a symmetrical panel of joined pieces of needlepoint.

3 Try on the cummerbund, wrong side out. Make any necessary adjustments to the fit. Note that there should be at least a small gap in between the two front edges in order to allow space for the eyes to be attached and for the lacing (which is the form of fastening on the cummerbund) to be threaded, see the photograph on page 80. Machine stitch the five adjoining sections of needlepoint together, taking in at least the very edge of the needlepoint so that no bare canvas will be visible. If you do not have access to a sewing machine then use backstitch instead (see the Techniques section, page 137). Also, if you wish to reduce the overall size of the cummerbund then you can do this by taking in more on the edges of the needlepoint. Press the seams open with the point of an iron. Note, do not iron directly on the needlepoint; protect the stitching with a cloth.

4 Place the lining fabric right side up on a flat surface. (I chose a soft blue cotton for the lining in order to complement the colours in the needlepoint. Feel free to select an alternative lightweight fabric for the lining if you prefer.) Place the needlepoint panel right side down on top of it. Pin the two layers together all around the edges of the needlepoint and cut out the lining fabric with a pair of sharp sewing scissors to the same size (b).

5 Baste the two layers together. Machine stitch around the side and lower edges of the cummerbund, leaving the top edge open. Once again, if you do not have access to a sewing machine then you can use a firm, neat backstitch (see Techniques, page 137). Note that machine stitching will be more secure. Trim the seam allowances to 1 cm (⅜ in) and also trim off the corners diagonally so as to reduce bulk on the finished piece. Turn the cummerbund right side out and use a knitting needle, or a similar object, to turn the seams out fully, especially in the corners. Baste around the stitched edges and press them with the point of an iron to flatten them. Remove the basting stitches. It is most important to flatten the perimeter of the cummerbund at this stage for a good result. Otherwise the seams may appear bulky and spoil the look of the finished piece.

6 Turn in the canvas and the lining along the top edge (c). Baste and then slipstitch these edges very neatly together (see Techniques, page 138). Place the cummerbund flat on a smooth, hard surface and lay some heavy books on top of it. Leave the cummerbund under these weights for at least several days. The pressure of the books will smoothe out any bulkiness and flatten all the seams nicely.

7 Insert six pins along each front edge of the lining and make sure that you space them evenly and position them so that they fall exactly opposite each other in properly aligned pairs. With neat hand stitches sew an eye at each position marked by a pin, working through the wrong side of the needlepoint. Make sure that each of the twelve eyes are fixed securely (d).

The final step is to thread the ribbon through the eyes in a criss-cross configuration, as shown in the photograph on page 80. I chose a narrow yellow velvet ribbon to complement the strong yellow in the tartans. You can choose any type of ribbon according to your taste and according to the colours in your chosen tartans, if you opt for a different pattern. It is entirely optional to add the kilt pin, but I think this touch is in keeping with the tartan theme. To wear the cummerbund, simply pull both ends of the ribbon up to an even length and tie them into a bow.

accessories

FLORAL EVENING BAG

Antique needlepoint bags are among the most beautiful examples of the art. The elaborate detail and intricacy in the work and the delicacy of craftsmanship displayed on some old pieces is quite stunning – some are stitched with as many as 1,000 stitches per square inch. These antique bags, which were once carried to the opera, theatre and to glittering social gatherings, are either in private collections or lie, for the most part, in museums. For instance, I have seen superb examples at the Burrell Collection in Glasgow. Fortunately, the tradition of carrying elegant evening bags to formal occasions survives to this day.

My family is lucky to have inherited a number of exquisite pieces of needlepoint which were designed and worked by my grandmother. One of these is the evening bag shown on page 6 and referred to in my introduction. I felt that it would be fun to design a contemporary needlepoint bag and I wanted to give it a modern shape, design and colour. So, I let my imagination go and experimented with rough shapes and hues in a floral pattern. I hugely enjoyed mixing colours and gauging the different effects that they had on each other. This free and spontaneous attitude to the design process meant that I did not worry about portraying my subject matter with great accuracy. The only restriction that I imposed upon myself was to keep within the outline of the flowers, which I drew straight onto the canvas. I was then able to enjoy working freely with the colours, stitching freehand within the outlines and choosing different threads as I went along. This is a very enjoyable way of working. Try it yourself, and you will be surprised how much you teach yourself about colour.

As an alternative, if you wish to make the whole design simpler and quicker, you could select just one colour for each flower. In this way you will end up with a bold bunch of flowers, which would have quite a different effect from this impressionistic style.

For this bag, I decided to work one side in needlepoint and cover the reverse side with fabric. I was lucky to find a piece of check silk in pastel colours to match those in the needlepoint. If you are feeling ambitious you could make both sides of the bag from needlepoint. Feel free to adapt my design and alter the colours. Or else create your own original design. If you do this note that the upper part of the needlepoint will be slightly gathered when the drawstrings are pulled, so avoid making the design very detailed, especially towards the top.

opposite: Inspired by my grandmother's fine evening bag (see page 6) I designed a contemporary equivalent on an impressionistic floral theme. (Caroline Robins)

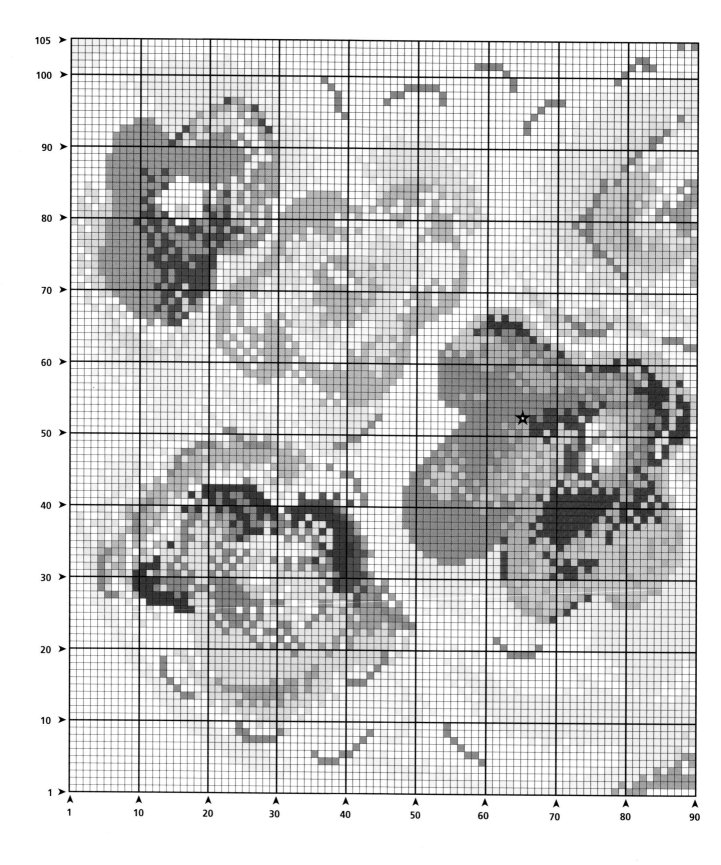

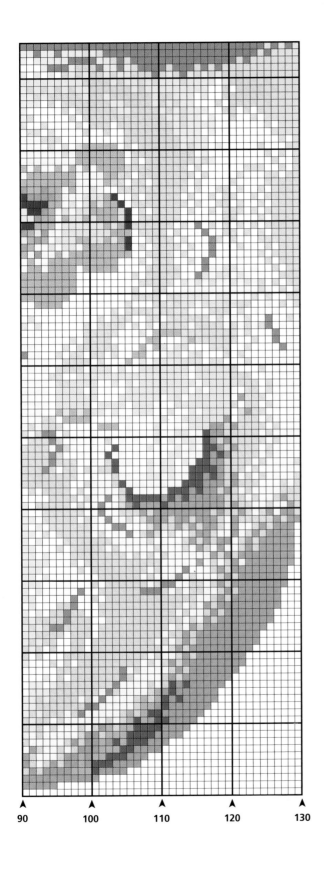

Use Anchor stranded cotton in the colours and quantities given in the key below. The initial numbers refer to the Anchor yarns; the numbers that follow in brackets refer to the number of skeins required. A 10 m (11 yd) skein will work approximately 900 stitches. (For DMC equivalents, see the conversion chart on page 140.)

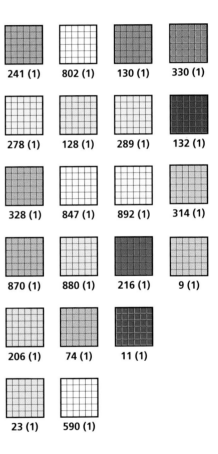

241 (1) 802 (1) 130 (1) 330 (1)

278 (1) 128 (1) 289 (1) 132 (1)

328 (1) 847 (1) 892 (1) 314 (1)

870 (1) 880 (1) 216 (1) 9 (1)

206 (1) 74 (1) 11 (1)

23 (1) 590 (1)

☆ **Mid-point of design**

90   100   110   120   130

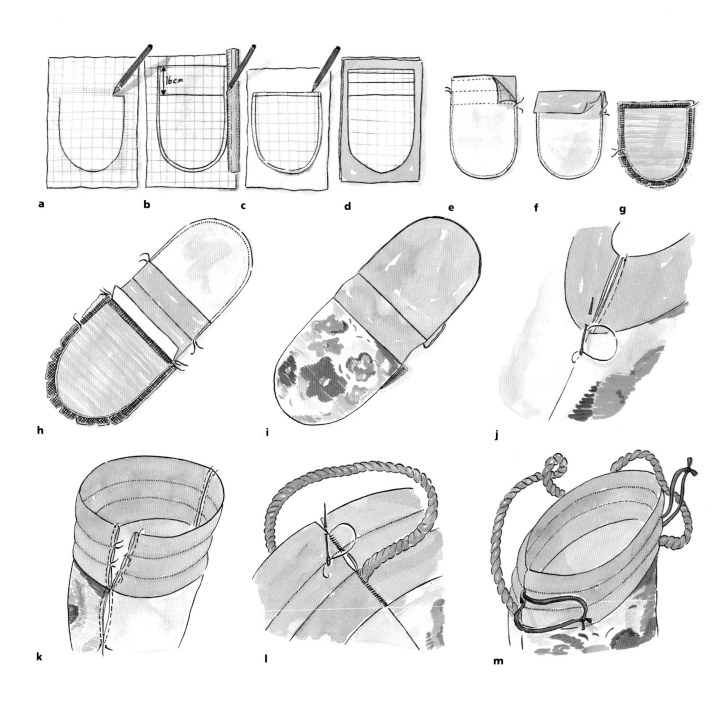

a   b   c   d   e   f   g

h   i   j

k   l   m

MATERIALS *&* EQUIPMENT

13-gauge canvas, 33 x 35 cm (13 x 14 in)

30 cm (⅜ yd) of backing fabric, such as

silk taffeta

40 cm (½ yd) of lining fabric

1.4 m (1½ yd) of decorative cord

1.5 m (1⅝ yd) of narrow decorative cord

for the drawstrings

Sewing thread to match the lining fabric

Tailor's chalk or fabric marker pen

Piece of paper measuring at least

42 x 28 cm (17 x 11 in)

Size 18 tapestry needle

The finished needlepoint measures

23 x 25.5 cm (9 x 10 in) and the bag

measures 30 x 25.5 cm (12 x 10 in)

Use all six strands of thread for stitching

Making up instructions

1 First block or stretch the finished needle-point. I strongly recommend that you have this done by a professional. However, if you choose to do it yourself at home, follow the instructions in the Techniques section on page 136. Trim the canvas edges to 2 cm (¾ in) all around.

2 Lay the sheet of paper over the wrong side of the needlepoint, positioning the lower edge near the bottom of the needlepoint. With a pencil, lightly trace around the edge of the stitched area (a). Remove the paper and smooth out the edges of the drawn outline. Use a ruler on the top edge to make it exactly straight. Extend the side edges upward for 16 cm (6½ in) and draw another line between them, parallel to the top edge. Finally, add 1 cm (½ in) all around the side and lower edges of the outline. Cut out this pattern (b).

3 Use the pattern to cut out two pieces of lining fabric (c). (I chose a silk taffeta, but feel free to select an alternative fabric, so long as it is of comparable weight to the needlepoint.) Trim off or fold down the pattern extension to within 1 cm (½ in) of the top edge. Use this shortened pattern to cut out one piece of the backing fabric (d); this should therefore be the same size as the needlepoint plus 1 cm (½ in) all around. Using tailor's chalk or a marker pen, lightly mark a line 2 cm (1 in) from the top, then two more lines 7 and 14 cm (2¾ and 5½ in) below that on the wrong side of the lining pieces. These mark the seam allowance, the top fold line and the position of top of the needlepoint, respectively.

4 Pin the two lining pieces together with right sides facing. Machine stitch them together from the top fold line on one side around to the position of the needlepoint on the other, taking in a 1 cm (½ in) seam allowance (e). If you do not have access to a sewing machine, you can use backstitch instead (see Techniques, page 137). Press the seam flat with the point of an iron up to the needlepoint position and press the seam open beyond this point.

5 Turn the lining fabric to the wrong side along the top fold line. Press in position. This doubled fabric will form the top extension of the bag (f).

6 Pin the needlepoint and backing piece together, with right sides facing. Baste and machine stitch, just inside the stitched area, leaving open the top edge and 10 cm (4 in) down one side. Use backstitch if you don't have a sewing machine. Trim the canvas edges to 1 cm (½ in). Notch the canvas along the curves with sharp sewing scissors, so as to reduce bulk (g). Press the seam open with the point of an iron. Do not iron directly on the needlepoint; protect with a cloth.

7 Pin the top edges of the needlepoint and the lining together, with right sides facing and with the longer unstitched edges of the lining on the same side as the open side edges of the bag (h). Baste and stitch, taking in the very edge of the needlepoint and 2 cm (1 in) of the lining. Trim the canvas to 1 cm (⅜ in). Press the seam allowances downward. Repeat to join the backing and the lining top edges.

8 Turn the bag right side out through the longer gap left in the side (i). Then push the

lining down inside the bag so that the pressed fold is positioned on top.

9 Turn under the seam allowances along the longer gap in the side and baste them in place. Then fold in the seam allowances on the shorter gap and baste them to the inner part of the lining.

10 Baste the free edges of the lining and the top extension together (j). Work two lines of stitching 2 cm and 3.5 cm (¾ in and 1⅜ in) below the fold from one edge to the other, to form a casing (k).

11 Slipstitch (see page 138) the edges of the shorter gap, beginning at the lower end and insert one end of the handle cord 1.5 cm (½ in) above the top edge of the needlepoint and backing. Sew it securely in place, leaving the casing edges open (l).

12 In the same way, slipstitch the longer gap edges together beginning on the inside and working around to the outside. Leave the casing edges open on the outside. Pin the free end of the braid to the bag in the same position as in the previous step. Adjust the length of the braid according to how you want to carry the bag. Insert the end into the seam and continue slipstitching to the end of the gap.

13 Cut the drawstring cord in two. Bind the ends with sticky tape in order to prevent fraying. Fasten a safety pin to one end of the cord (or thread it into a bodkin) and insert it into one of the casing openings. Take it all the way through the casing, then remove the tape and knot the two ends together. Repeat with the other cord, inserting it into the other opening (m). Pull on the cords to close the bag.

NDEBELE DUFFLE BAG

The Ndebele tribe (pronounced "En de *bay* lay") live in South Africa in the Transvaal district. They are a nomadic tribe who have suffered terribly under apartheid; they have been herded off their land into "resettlement camps", where they don't have enough pasture to farm properly and they have to travel long distances to work. Yet through all their hardships, the Ndebele have managed to cling tenaciously to their art and craft.

The style of the Ndebele is instantly recognizable by its strong colours and dynamic geometric shapes. The first time I saw their work I was astounded by its boldness and daring use of colour. A distinctive technique they use is a sharp black outline to delineate the shapes while the colours are applied totally flat. Many of the shapes appear at first glance to be abstract patterns, but if you look closer, you'll spot such objects as lightbulbs, houses, windows, planes and even razor blades. It's a curious vocabulary which is continually being expanded; as a new generation of artists is introduced to the art, they re-interpret the symbols and modify them, adding their own embellishments, such as lightning flashes or animals, and sometimes they abstract the original motifs beyond recognition. The colours traditionally used by the Ndebele came from the earth and the clays found in their region – reds, ochres, browns and black, the latter derived from soot. Today, modern commercial paints are available and offer a wider choice of colours and are more durable than the natural pigments, which need re-applying regularly, especially after a downpour.

I had been thinking about a project based on a Ndebele theme and I wanted to make something decorative but functional and so decided on a bag. I liked the idea of a frieze running around a basic shape, to echo the way that the Ndebele decorate the walls of their houses with murals. The colouring took a lot of thought – should it be extravagant to reflect recent Ndebele work, or should it reflect their older colour spectrum? In the end I tried to combine the two themes and chose rich browns, a couple of shades of blue and an electric tangerine to add some spark. I also used a strong black outline. The angles and shapes that recur in Ndebele patterns transferred perfectly onto the canvas grid.

Try to develop your own geometric vocabulary. Start by working with a ruler and a 45° set square on graph paper and progress to freehand, stitching along the lines of the canvas. All Ndebele art is executed freehand and worked straight onto a surface to give the design a dynamism of its own.

opposite: To recreate the idea of a Ndebele mural, I designed a frieze of geometric shapes in rich colours around a practical duffle bag. (Christine Büttner)

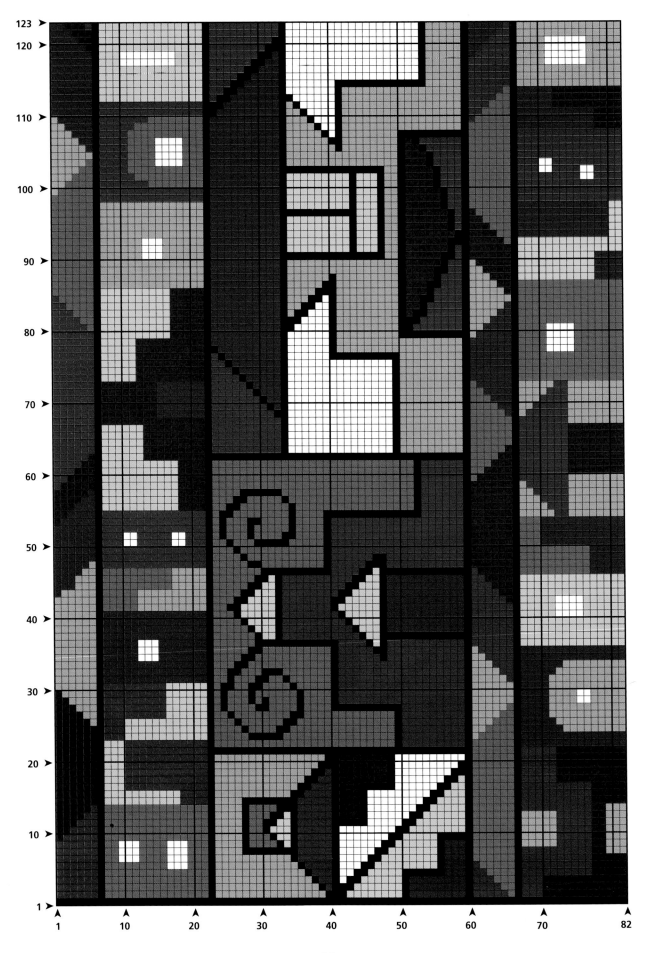

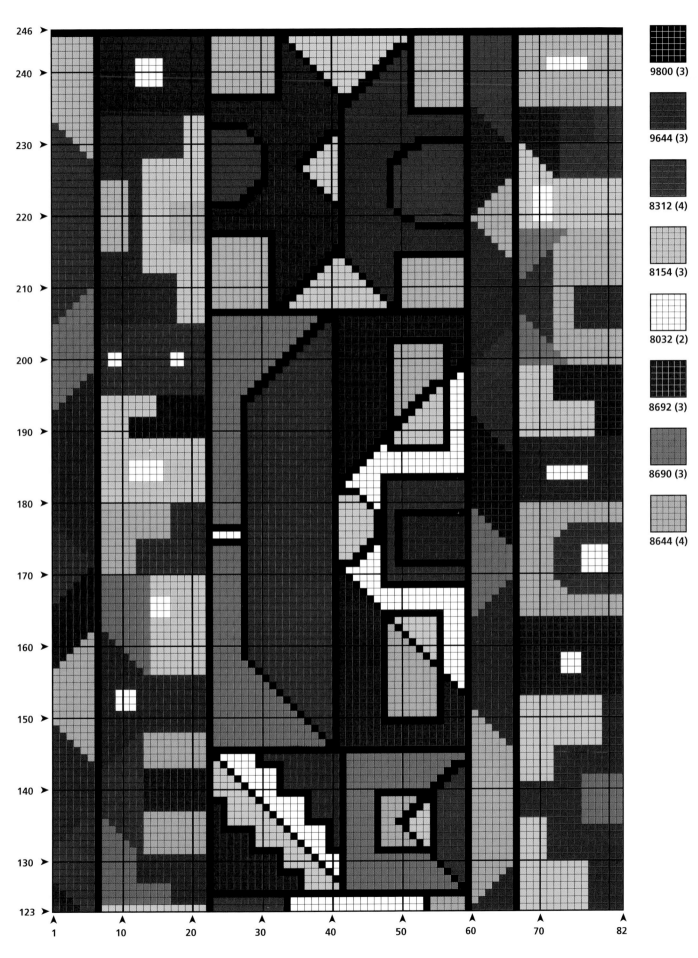

9800 (3)

9644 (3)

8312 (4)

8154 (3)

8032 (2)

8692 (3)

8690 (3)

8644 (4)

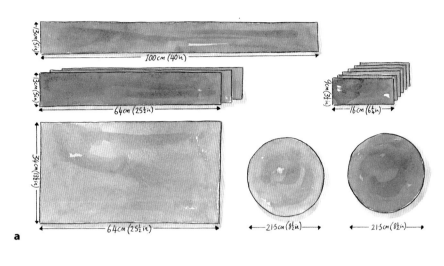

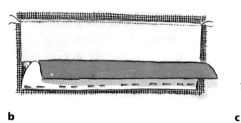

a

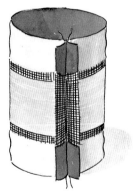

b

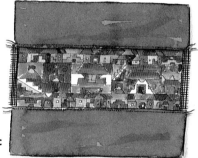

c

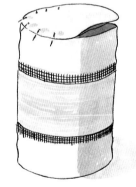

e

See the previous pages for the chart. Use Anchor wool in the colours and quantities given in the key on the previous page. The initial numbers refer to the Anchor yarns; the numbers that follow in brackets refer to the number of skeins required. A 10 m (11 yd) skein will work approximately 950 stitches. (For DMC equivalents, see the conversion chart on page 141.)

MATERIALS & EQUIPMENT

10-gauge canvas, 72 x 31 cm (28½ x 12 in)

60 cm (⅝ yd) of heavyweight fabric, such as wool, cotton or velvet; if the fabric is less than 100 cm (40 in) wide, the handle will need to be pieced

40 cm (⅜ yd) of medium-weight lining fabric

Black sewing thread

Size 18 tapestry needle

Compass

The finished needlepoint measures 21 x 62 cm (8¼ x 24½ in); the finished bag, is about 43 cm (17 in) deep and 19 cm (7½ in) in diameter

Use one strand of yarn for stitching

d

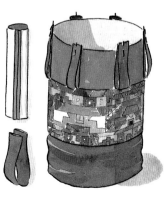

f

g

h

Making up instructions

1 First block or stretch the finished needle-point. I strongly recommend that you have this done by a professional. However, if you choose to do it yourself at home, follow the instructions in the Techniques section on page 136. Trim the canvas edges to 2 cm (¾ in) all around.

2 Cut out all the necessary fabric pieces for the bag. For the main fabric, choose a heavyweight cloth such as a velvet to complement the colours in the needlepoint design. Cut out the following: three rectangles, each one should measure 13 x 64 cm (5 x 25½ in); six strips for the loops, each one should measure 16 x 9 cm (6¼ x 3½ in) and one strip for the handle, measuring 100 x 13 cm (40 x 5 in). Set the compass to a radius of 10.7 cm (4¼ in) and use it to draw a circle on a sheet of paper. Using this outline as a pattern, cut out a circle of main fabric which will form the bottom of the bag. For the lining, choose a medium-weight fabric in a colour that complements the main fabric and the needlepoint. Cut out a rectangle measuring 34 x 64 cm (13½ x 25½ in) and a circle using the pattern already used for cutting out the circle of main fabric. Follow the templates shown in the illustration (a) to ensure accurate measuring.

3 Place one rectangle of the main fabric right side down along the upper edge of the needlepoint, so that the fabric edge extends 1 cm (⅜ in) past the stitching along the top and sides. If you are using velvet, position the fabric so that the nap will run downward when the fabric is turned right side up. (The nap is a pile or finish on the

fabric surface that lies in one direction only. If two pieces of fabric are joined with the nap facing in different directions the piece with the nap lying the wrong way will appear lighter. To determine the direction of the nap brush your hand across the fabric to see which way the pile lies smoothly.)

Pin, baste and machine stitch along the top edge, just inside the stitched area (b). If you do not have access to a sewing machine, use backstitch instead (see page 137). Note that machine stitching will be stronger than hand stitching. Join another rectangle to the lower edge of the needlepoint in the same way. Again, if you are using velvet, take care to position the nap correctly. Open out both fabric pieces and press the seam flat with the point of an iron (c). Topstitch 5 mm (¼ in) from the seams, see Techniques page 138.

4 Place the two short edges of the bag together, with right sides facing. Pin, baste and stitch, taking a 1 cm (½ in) seam allowance in the fabric and catching in the very edges of the needlepoint to prevent any canvas threads from showing (d).

5 Pin the bottom piece to the lower edge of the bag (e) with right sides facing (make sure that it is the lower edge so that the needlepoint will be the right way up). Baste and then machine stitch, or backstitch, taking a 1 cm (⅜ in) seam allowance. Turn the bag right side out.

6 To make the loops that are attached around the mouth of the bag, fold each strip in half lengthways and stitch 1 cm (⅜ in) from the long edges. Press the seam open with the point of an iron. Turn the

strip right side out and press it flat with the point of an iron, so that the seam lies in the middle down one side and is not visible on the other side. Fold each loop in half width-ways, with the seam on the inside and pin the loops around the mouth of the bag, spacing each one evenly (f).

7 Join the remaining rectangle (which forms the facing) along its two short ends. Place it over the mouth of the bag with the right sides facing and the raw edges matching (g). You will need to ease the bag slightly to fit the facing. Baste, then machine stitch or backstitch 1 cm (⅜ in) from the edges. Trim the bag seam allowance close to the stitching in order to reduce bulk, then turn the velvet facing to the inside of the bag. Press the top edge of the bag.

8 Join the rectangle of medium-weight lining fabric along the short ends. Press the seam open with the point of an iron. Join the bottom piece to one end. Turn under 1 cm (⅜ in) on the top edge and machine stitch or backstitch this hem in place.

9 Leaving the lining turned wrong side out, place it inside the bag. Make sure that it fits the bottom snugly: the top edge should just overlap the lower edge of the facing. Pin and baste the top edge over the velvet facing. Slipstitch the lining in place (see page 138) working the needle through the facing and the seam allowance underneath.

10 Make the handle as for the loops, see step 6. Thread the finished handle through each of the loops. Join the open ends by slipping one end into the other. Turn under the raw edge on the outer end and machine stitch across the joined ends (h).

BLACK AND WHITE PURSE

This little purse and the matching buttons evolved out of a series of test pieces, which involved looking at the different types of pattern that could be achieved by following the vertical and horizontal construction of the canvas. In other words, the pattern is a strictly grid-based design. In order to retain the crisp quality of the patterns within the overall design, I decided to limit myself to two contrasting tones: black and white, or rather cream, which I prefer to bright white because it is a little softer and warmer.

In terms of the colour spectrum these two tones are not real colours – black is the total absorption of all colours and white, by contrast, is a blend of all colour wavelengths. The two set each other off perfectly and the strong impact of this classic combination has been exploited by designers, artists and craftsmen since time immemorial. To cite a few examples, the combination appears in ancient Greek and Roman mosaics, in the chequerboard marble tile floors seen in some 17th-century Dutch paintings, in Elizabethan blackwork embroidery, with its delicate floral and abstract patterns, and in the giddy Op Art of the 1960s. Likewise, in the fashion industry, black and white is a perennial theme and one which seems timeless, ageless and perpetually elegant.

In my professional design work I often use black and white and I thought that it would be fun to make some black and white needlepoint accessories for a winter coat. I don't like to have loose change or wayward pieces of jewellery jangling around in the bottom of my handbag, which swallows things up all too often, and pockets are not very secure. So, I thought that a little purse that could be attached to a belt would be an ideal way to carry small items conveniently. This project is an appropriate one for a beginner to tackle – it requires just two shades of yarn and is on a small scale and so it is relatively quick and easy to complete.

Originally I was going to cover the purse with just one overall design. But after trying out some variations I decided that it would be visually more interesting to make a patchwork out of the different patterns, particularly as I wanted to work in duo-tone. If you prefer, you could stitch the purse in a different combination of colours, perhaps choosing shades to match a bag that you already possess. You could use either a two-colour scheme or select different colour combinations for each block of the pattern for a more colourful result. Because this is a small project, use a small-gauge canvas to allow maximum detail in the design.

opposite: A small-scale project which is ideal for beginners. This purse is composed of just two shades of yarn and constructed on a strict grid-based design. (Christine Büttner)

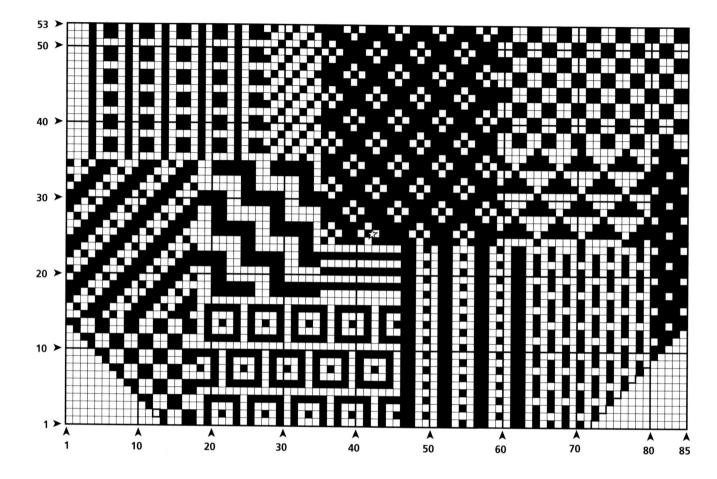

Use Anchor stranded cotton in the colours and quantities given in the key on the right. The initial numbers refer to the Anchor yarns; the numbers that follow in brackets refer to the number of skeins required. An 8 m (9 yd) skein will work approximately 1,150 stitches. (For DMC equivalents, see the conversion chart on page 140.)

403 (2)   275 (2)

☆ Mid-point of design

MATERIALS & EQUIPMENT

16-gauge canvas, 20 x 23 cm (8 x 9 in), preferably double thread canvas

20 cm (¼ yd) of black cotton or silk fabric for lining and backing

Bead, button or press stud or snap for fastening

Black sewing thread

Size 22 tapestry needle

Tailor's pencil or chalk

Measures 10 x 13 cm (4 x 5 in)

Use all six strands of thread for stitching

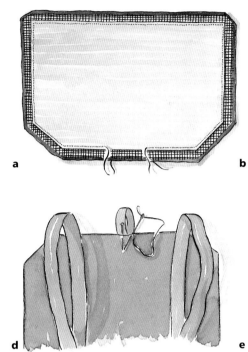

a

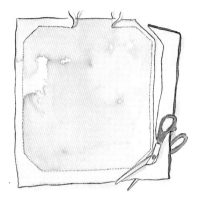

b

c

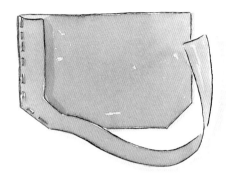

d

e

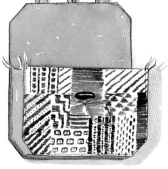

f

Making up instructions

1 Block the needlepoint (see page 136). Trim the canvas to 1 cm (⅜ in) all around.

2 From the lining/backing fabric cut out the inside front lining, 10.5 x 16 cm (4¼ x 6¼ in); two back pieces, each 17 x 16 cm (6¾ x 6¼ in); gusset 31x 7 cm (12¼ x 2¾ in); two loops, each 30 x 5 cm (12 x 2 in); fastening loop for bead or button, 6 x 3 cm (2½ x 1¼ in).

3 Pin the needlepoint and the front lining with right sides facing. Baste and machine stitch just inside the needlepoint, leaving a 7 cm (½ in) gap in the lower edge (a).

4 Trim the canvas and lining edges to 5 mm (¼ in). Trim the corners. Turn right side out.

5 Turn in the edges along the gap and slipstitch together (see page 138). Press.

6 Pin the two back pieces with right sides facing. With tailor's pencil trace around the lower edge of the front piece at the top and bottom edges of the back to reproduce the shape. Machine stitch the two back pieces along the marked line, leaving a 7 cm (2½ in) gap in the top edge (b).

7 Trim the seam allowance to 5 mm (¼ in). Turn right side out. Turn in the edges along the gap, but do not stitch. Press.

8 Fold each of the belt loops in half lengthways, with right sides facing. Stitch 5 mm (¼ in) from the long edges and one short end. Turn each strip right side out. Press.

9 Fold each strip in half. Place the unfinished end under the finished one, pin each loop to the back of the purse 3 cm (1 ¼ in) from the bottom and side edges. Topstitch the loops in a rectangle 5 cm (2 in) long (c).

10 If you are using a button or bead, stitch the loop as for the belt loops, see step 8.

Fold it in half; insert the ends into the gap along the top edge of the back piece, leaving 2 cm (¾ in) of loop outside. Pin in place. Slipstitch the edges of the gap, taking in the loop (d). To fasten with a press stud, just slipstitch the gap edges together.

11 Prepare the gusset as for the loops, see step 8. Press. Beginning with the finished end, pin and baste it to the side and bottom edges of the front section (e). Trim the remaining end, if necessary, turn in the edges and slipstich together. Stitch the gusset and front together by machine or by hand. Repeat to join the gusset to the back.

12 Fold the back flap over the front and press. Mark the position for the bead or button and sew it in place (f). Or sew a press stud to the inside edge of the flap and to a corresponding position on the purse front.

BUTTONS AND TIE PINS

If you have completed one or more of the projects in the clothing section, or finished a project in the accessories chapter, you may like to complement your efforts so far by making some buttons, tie pins or brooches. These small-scale needlepoint items are delightful to make, you can copy my designs overleaf or invent your own to go with garments in your wardrobe. Or, if you are a beginner to the craft, then what better than to take up needlepoint with a button or tie pin as a starting point? These are quick to make and the metal casings are easy to assemble. They are available from haberdashery or notions departments and come in several sizes. Although they are intended to be covered with fabric, why not use needlepoint instead? I had most success with the largest size, 38 mm (1½ in) in diameter, which allows for greater detail than smaller sizes. Although my black and white buttons illustrated on page 101 are ideally suited to the 30 mm (1¼ in) size.

Small items such as these are an ideal way to test out a design idea before you launch into a major, time-consuming project. In a matter of a few hours you can experiment with colour and imagery and still produce something attractive and useful. Small-scale projects also present the challenge of seeing how much detail you can incorporate into the design. I look upon the task as similar to that of designing postage stamps! You can turn to a host of different sources for button design, see the chapter on design inspiration for guidance, pages 11-17.

All these buttons are worked on 18-gauge canvas, to allow for some detail, without being dauntingly intricate. You should use stranded cotton to give lustre and clear definition. If you wish to design your own buttons it is important to remember that the needlepoint must measure slightly more than the diameter of the button as some will be needed to cover the edges. For a 38 mm (1½ in) diameter button I allowed a margin of 3 mm (⅛ in), so a total of 6 mm (¼ in) was added so that the overall diameter of the needlepoint was 44 cm (1¾ in).

I now have a growing collection of buttons as they are so satisfying to make and can transform any item of clothing. They can be used in all sorts of ways – I have used one to decorate a hat and another to replace a dull fastening on a handbag. Try converting buttons into earrings or brooches by removing the wire shank from the back and replacing it with the appropriate jewellery fastening. You can even frame buttons and display them as tiny works of art!

opposite: Buttons and tie pins are quick and simple to make. You can copy these geometric designs or else invent your own to complement your wardrobe. (Christine Büttner)

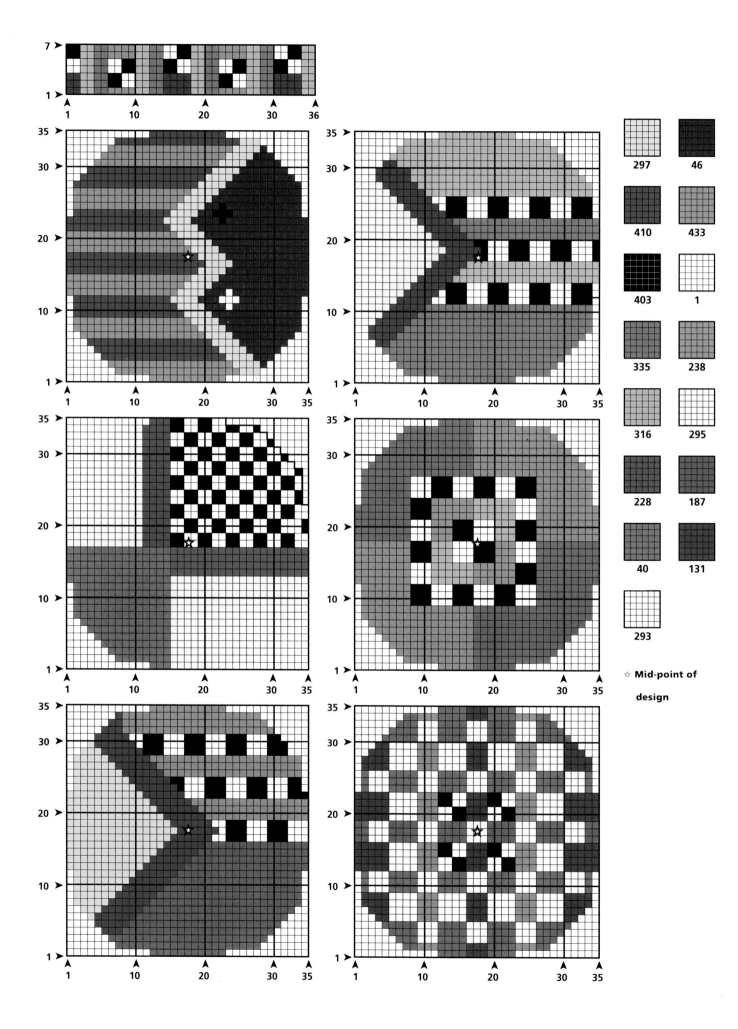

297 46
410 433
403 1
335 238
316 295
228 187
40 131
293

☆ Mid-point of design

a

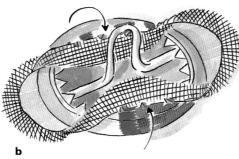

b

c

The numbers in the key opposite refer to the Anchor stranded cottons. (For DMC equivalents, see the conversion chart on page 140.) One skein of each colour is enough to work all the buttons and the tie pin.

MATERIALS & EQUIPMENT

18-gauge canvas, approximately 13 cm (5 in) square for each button

Buttons and tie pin kits

Size 22 tapestry needle

All-purpose glue

Small pliers or tweezers

The buttons measure approximately 3 and 4 cm (1¼ and 1½ in) in diameter

Use all six strands of thread for stitching

Making up instructions

1 For the buttons: block the needlepoint (see page 136). Trim the canvas edges to about 2-2.5 cm (¾-1 in) all around.

2 Place the needlepoint face down on a smooth, hard surface. Position the button form on top and centre it over the work (a). Pull the canvas up over the edges, first on one side and then on the opposite side and fasten it over the teeth (b). Continue, working on opposite sides alternately so as to keep the work straight and centred, until the edges are firmly attached. Trim any spare canvas if necessary.

3 Press the back of the button down over the canvas. It should snap firmly into place (c). If not, trim the canvas and try again.

1 For the tie pin: block the needlepoint (see page 136). Trim the canvas edges to 3 mm (⅛ in) all around.

2 Place a very small blob of glue on the flat middle section of the kit. Position the needlepoint over this, making sure that it is exactly centred, with the canvas extending evenly over the sides (a). Leave it to dry.

3 Position the framing piece over the backed needlepoint (b) and press the two together so the needlepoint fits snugly in the frame. Trim off any stray canvas ends.

4 Position the clip or pin correctly in relation to the design and the way that the tie pin will be attached. Place the back panel in position. With the pliers or tweezers bend the prongs over the back (c).

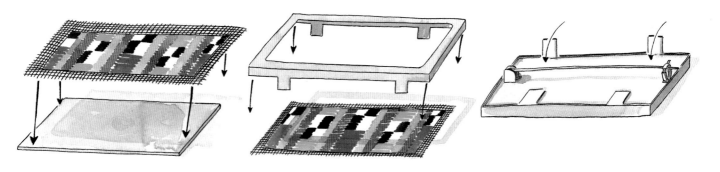

a

b

c

STARBURST SPECTACLES CASE

The inspiration behind this design came from a film project that I was working on. It was an animation designed around a newly commissioned piece of music and I was trying to reflect the sound of the instruments in the colours and shapes of the visuals. The music was a rhythmic, lively piece and I felt that the colours should be bright and full of zest to complement this. After attentive listening to the music I struck upon my colour combination: the yellow to represent the brass section; the blue the wind instruments and the pink the human voice, which was vibrant and distinct above the other sounds.

The symbolism and psychology of colours is a fascinating and complex subject. For example, while red is often used to represent danger, it is also the colour of love and passion, and in Russian the word for red also means "beautiful". Leonardo da Vinci declared that yellow represents the earth, whereas for the ancient Greeks it symbolized the air. Once you begin to delve into colour symbolism your eyes will be opened to a freshly coloured world.

If you have a favourite piece of music then you could try an abstract interpretation in needlepoint. Use warm, fiery colours to reflect drama and crescendo and cool blues and pastels for quieter interludes.

Another aspect of colour which I exploited in this project is the way that translucent colours react and change when they are laid one over another – hence the multi-coloured shadows and gradations of shading where the colours meet and cross. Of course this piece of needlepoint doesn't pretend to be scientifically accurate, but I had great fun experimenting with the spectrum. To prepare for the design I gathered together different shades of semi-transparent tissue paper. By placing these over each other and holding them up to the light I could devise all kinds of unusual colour effects.

On the whole I find spectacles and sunglasses cases rather unimaginative items and I thought that I would make one that was more arresting, something to display instead of just throwing into a pocket or a handbag. I padded the case to protect the spectacles and to add to the tactile quality.

The opaque, miniature beads that border three sides of the case echo the pink dots in the design and give the piece a jewel-like quality which contrasts with the texture of the needlepoint. Beads figure prominently in the adornment of crafts the world over, from the American Indian to some African tribes, and they are often used today to embellish modern embroidery.

opposite: My starburst spectacles case was originally inspired by a piece of music, hence its abstract design. I used beads to border the case for a contrast in texture. (Christine Büttner)

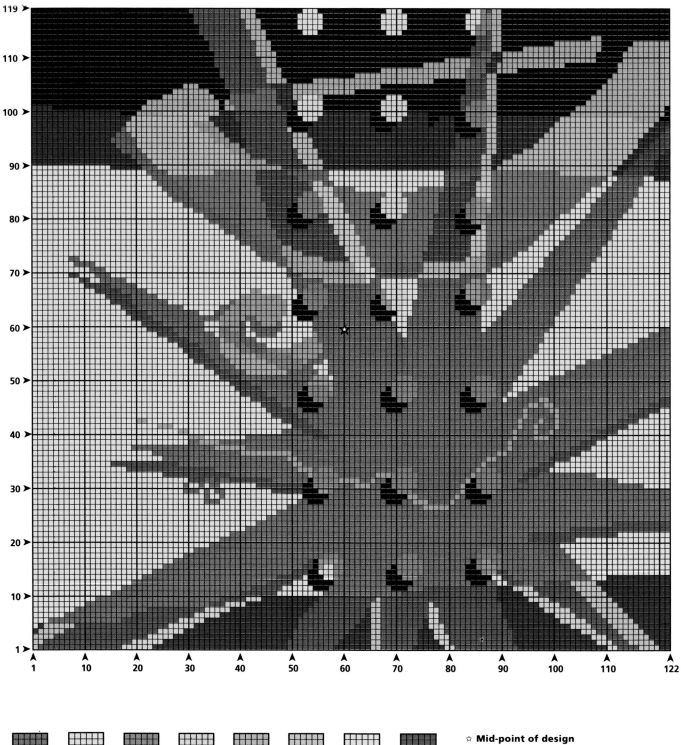

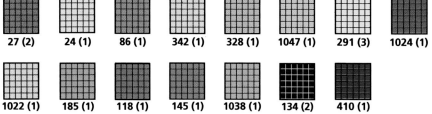

27 (2)	24 (1)	86 (1)	342 (1)	328 (1)	1047 (1)	291 (3)	1024 (1)

☆ **Mid-point of design**

1022 (1)	185 (1)	118 (1)	145 (1)	1038 (1)	134 (2)	410 (1)

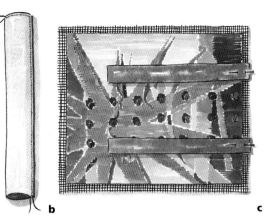

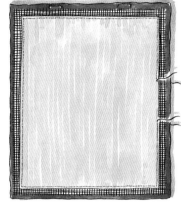

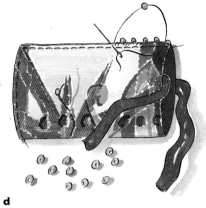

a   b   c   d

Use Anchor stranded cotton in the colours and quantities given in the key opposite. The initial numbers refer to the Anchor yarns; the numbers that follow in brackets refer to the number of skeins required. An 8 m (9 yd) skein will work approximately 1,280 stitches. (For DMC equivalents, see the conversion chart on page 140.)

MATERIALS & EQUIPMENT

17-gauge canvas, 23 cm (11 in) square

20 cm (¼ yd) of soft cotton or silk for the lining and ties

Piece of lightweight wadding, 16 x 15 cm (6¼ x 6 in)

30-40 small beads (optional)

Sewing thread to match the lining fabric

Size 22 tapestry needle

Measures about 17 x 8 cm (6½ x 3 in)

Use all six strands of thread for stitching

Making up instructions

1 First block or stretch the finished needlepoint. I strongly recommend that you have this done by a professional. However, if you choose to do it yourself at home, follow the instructions in the Techniques section on page 136. Trim the canvas edges to 1 cm (⅜ in) all around.

2 From the soft cotton or silk lining fabric cut out one rectangular piece measuring 19.5 x 19 cm (7¾ x 7½ in) and two strips, each one measuring 16.5 x 3 cm (6½ x 1¼ in).

3 To make the ties to fasten the spectacles case, fold each strip in half lengthways with the right sides facing. Pin and machine stitch close to the long edges and across one end (a). If you do not have access to a sewing machine, use backstitch instead, see page 137. Turn each strip right side out. Press with the point of an iron.

4 Lay the needlepoint right side up. Pin the two ties along the top edge of the design, positioning each one approximately 3.5 cm (1⅜ in) in from the outer edges (b). Baste them securely to the canvas edges. Place the lining on top, right side down. Pin and baste it in place, then machine stitch or

backstitch, taking in the very edge of the needlepoint. You should stitch in order to prevent any bare canvas from showing and also catch in the ties. Leave a gap of approximately 10 cm (4 in) in the middle of one long edge (c).

5 Trim off the lining and canvas close to the edge of the stitching and also trim away the corners diagonally to reduce bulk on the finished piece . Turn the case right side out. Use a knitting needle or a similar object to turn the seams right side out fully. Press the edges well with the point of an iron to make them crisp.

6 Insert the piece of wadding through the gap left in step 4. Ease it inside and make sure that it lies flat, then slipstitch the gap edges together (see page 138).

7 Fold the spectacles case in half. Pin and baste, making sure that the edges are even and align properly. Slipstitch the edges together (d), taking very small stitches (see page 138). Refer back to the photograph of the finished project on page 109 and, if you like the border of beads, incorporate a bead every 7 mm (¼ in) or so around the perimeter with neat hand stitches.

gifts

CHRISTMAS DECORATIONS

Every year unpacking the Christmas box is like a trip back into our family history. For as long as I can remember, each Christmas we have added something new to the tree and so it is loaded with memories. The earliest addition I can recall are a pair of felt reindeer heads. Then there was the year of the peg dolls, when my mother made a host of fairies and a Father Christmas to perch on the branches among the tinsel and baubles. And another year there were birds with beautiful silver and gold trailing tails. This family tradition of adding new decorations to the tree each year continues to this day and it is a custom I hope to continue in the future. I also like the idea of giving close friends things that I've made especially for them, and making Christmas tree decorations seems the perfect opportunity. These projects are quite small and so they are particularly suitable for the beginner, or for those who may be short of time.

I began to design these pieces of needlepoint in my usual way, doing lots of experimental doodles to work out the shapes and symbols. I wanted to avoid the usual Christmas symbols such as bunches of holly and angels. Instead, I sought a group of shapes with a more general appeal that could in fact be called into use at any time of the year, for birthdays, anniversaries and even weddings. Eventually I settled on a fish, a bird, a star and a heart. Each of these images, of course, carries certain connotations. The fish is a symbol of Christianity and it seems to have become a popular motif with many contemporary craftsmen; the bird also has religious links, with Noah and the Ark for example, but it also represents freedom and peace. The heart, suggesting love and harmony, is one of those images that is universally recognized and it crops up in many cultures, from traditional Scandinavian embroideries to the famous "I love New York" logo. The star is the image which is most directly related to Christmas and evokes the Star of Bethlehem.

When it came to deciding which colours to use I deliberately avoided the ubiquitous Yuletide red and green and looked instead for something a little more unexpected. So, after hours of playing with my skeins of thread I settled on the palette that you see opposite. You could try out your own colourways, or design your own shapes – a dog or a cat, perhaps, or a flower. Keep the outlines simple so that you can turn them right side out. Whatever you decide to stitch, you should enjoy the results for many Christmases and special occasions to come.

opposite: A collection of Christmas decorations which can be attached to a tree with long ribbons; they can also be used for birthdays and other special occasions. (Christine Büttner)

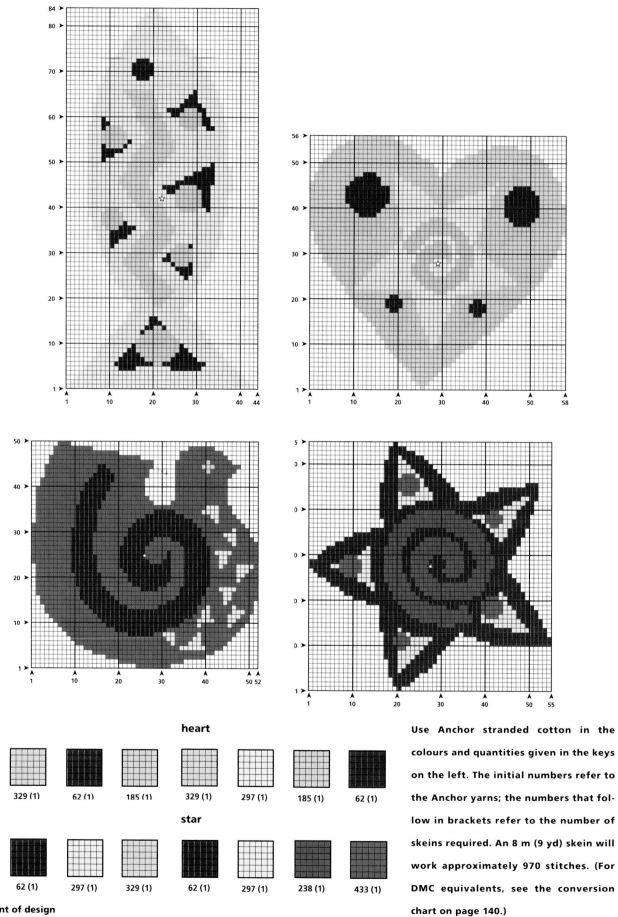

fish

297 (2)   329 (1)   62 (1)   185 (1)

bird

433 (2)   62 (1)   297 (1)   329 (1)

heart

329 (1)   297 (1)   185 (1)   62 (1)

star

62 (1)   297 (1)   238 (1)   433 (1)

☆ **Mid-point of design**

Use Anchor stranded cotton in the colours and quantities given in the keys on the left. The initial numbers refer to the Anchor yarns; the numbers that follow in brackets refer to the number of skeins required. An 8 m (9 yd) skein will work approximately 970 stitches. (For DMC equivalents, see the conversion chart on page 140.)

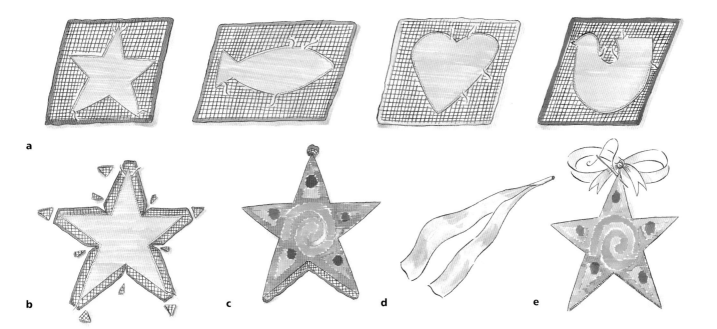

a

b   c   d   e

MATERIALS & EQUIPMENT

14-gauge canvas, 12 x 60 cm (5 x 24 in)

for all four decorations

Soft backing fabric for each decoration,

12 cm (5 in) square. Backing fabric 10 x

18 cm (4 x 7 in) for the fish

80 cm (⅞ yd) of ribbon, 2-4 cm (¾ -1½ in)

wide, for each decoration

Polyester fibrefill

Sewing thread to match backing fabrics

Size 22 tapestry needle

Measure 6-9 cm (2½ x 3½ in) in height

Use all six strands of thread for stitching

Making up instructions

1 First block or stretch the finished needlepoint. I strongly recommend that you have this done by a professional. However, if you choose to do it yourself at home, follow the instructions in the Techniques section on page 136. Block each of the needlepoint shapes individually.

2 Place the piece of needlepoint on the soft backing fabric, right sides together. Pin and baste them together, then machine stitch or backstitch (see page 137) around the shape, just inside the needlepoint, leaving two gaps: a smaller one for inserting the ribbon and a larger one for turning the shape right side out (a).

3 Trim the canvas and fabric edges to approximately 5 mm (¼ in) all around. With a pair of sharp sewing scissors snip into the corners and curves and also cut diagonally across the points or corners in order to reduce the bulk of the finished piece (b).

Turn each shape right side out and poke out the corners with the aid of a knitting needle or a pair of tweezers (c).

4 Fold the ribbon in half widthways, then make another fold in the folded end to make it narrower. Secure this with a few hand stitches to hold it in place (d). Insert the folded end of the ribbon into the smaller gap. Sew it in place firmly and close the gap with tiny oversewing stitches (see page 138) working through all the layers, so that when the stuffing is inserted none of it will be able to creep out.

5 Stuff the decoration with the polyester fibrefill, making sure that all the points and corners are evenly filled.

6 Turn in the raw edges of the needlepoint and backing fabric and pin them together. Sew them together neatly with tiny oversewing stitches. Trim the end of each ribbon and tie into a bow, leaving a loop for hanging the decoration on the Christmas tree (e).

LEMON COASTER

To complement the two following projects, the tomato placemat (see page 123) and the pea napkin ring (see page 126), I decided to make this lemon coaster. All three designs were inspired by a trip to a French market in Menton on the Côte d'Azur in the South of France. Fruit and vegetables provide a rich source of ideas as they offer an abundance of shape, colour and texture to the would-be needlepoint designer. In all three projects I have tried to convey the subject matter in a painterly way, using subtle variations of yarns to provide gradations of shades. I chose the colours for all three projects in relation to each other: the bright, acid yellow of the lemon coaster blends with the fresh green of the pea napkin ring, which in turn complements the summery green and red in the tomato placemat. The idea was to create a delicious-looking table setting before the addition of the food.

I have always found the gorgeous still-life paintings associated with the 17th-century Dutch artists such as Jan Brueghel a wonderful source of inspiration. All the fruits and vegetables in them look so sensuous and have extraordinary depth of colour. I wanted my lemon to evoke this type of fruit rather than the more uniform, waxy lemons that are normally found in supermarkets. I much

prefer the large, bulbous ones that you see hanging on trees in Mediterranean countries, which give off a glorious citrus scent. In Menton, there is even a lemon festival held every year in February.

So, I began to create my own version of a lemon. A cross-section seemed the obvious choice for a coaster, but I avoided making it a perfect circle, so as to suggest the pleasing irregularity that I prefer. I had great fun adding a range of shades and even included greens and blues to create more depth.

If you prefer, you could choose a different fruit or a vegetable for a coaster. For instance, you might like to attempt a cross-section of an orange, a kiwi or a passion fruit, or keep the fruit whole and work an apple or a pear in needlepoint – for any of these ideas you should be able to find quick and easy reference with a single trip to your local greengrocer or supermarket. You could also adapt one of the tomatoes from the placemat, using the finer-gauge canvas and the stranded cotton, as for the lemon coaster. Begin by drawing a circle of the chosen size on the canvas with a needlepoint pen. Then trace the tomato from the placemat and transfer the outline to canvas. When you have finished stitching the main fruit, just fill in the background with a chosen colour.

opposite: This lemon coaster is like a drop of strong sunlight on a table. You can use all kinds of fruits in cross-section to the same effect. (Caroline Robins)

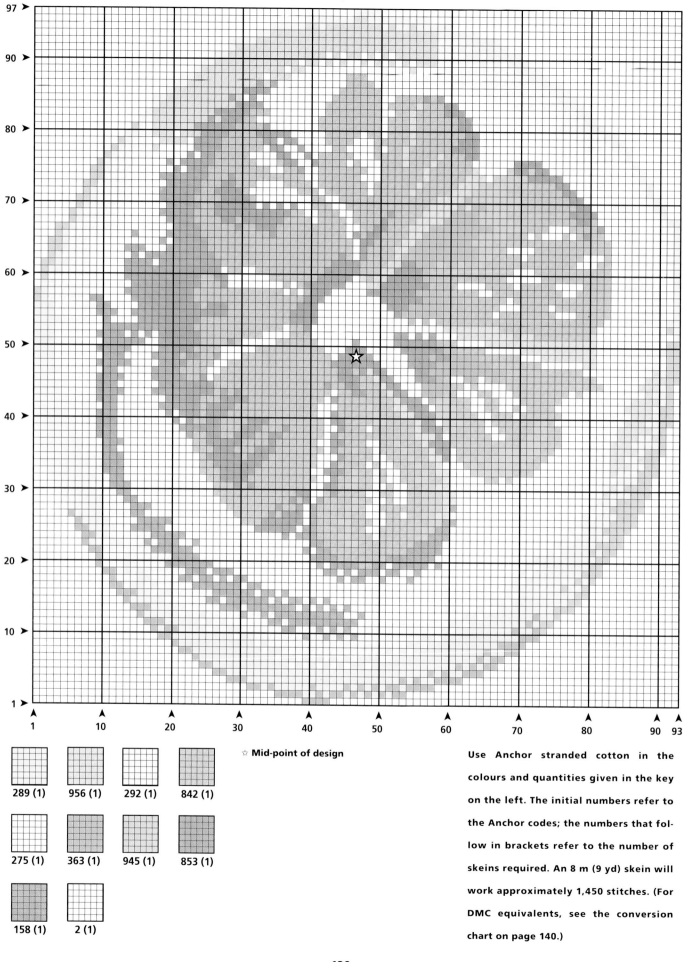

☆ **Mid-point of design**

289 (1) 956 (1) 292 (1) 842 (1)

275 (1) 363 (1) 945 (1) 853 (1)

158 (1) 2 (1)

Use Anchor stranded cotton in the colours and quantities given in the key on the left. The initial numbers refer to the Anchor codes; the numbers that follow in brackets refer to the number of skeins required. An 8 m (9 yd) skein will work approximately 1,450 stitches. (For DMC equivalents, see the conversion chart on page 140.)

a

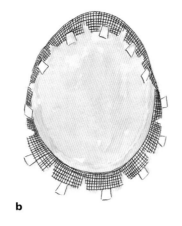

b

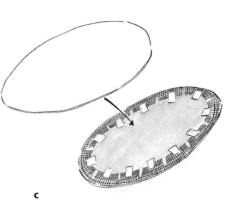

c

MATERIALS & EQUIPMENT

18-gauge canvas, 24 cm (9½ in) square

Thin hardboard or particle board, at least

17 cm (6½ in) square, for the backing

Coping saw

Medium-grade sandpaper

Adhesive tape

Strong fabric glue

Felt backing fabric, 17 cm (6½ in) square

Size 20 tapestry needle

Measures about 14.5 x 13 cm (5¾ x 5 in)

Use all six strands of thread for stitching

Making up instructions

1 First block or stretch the finished needle-point. I strongly recommend that you have this done by a professional. However, if you choose to do it yourself at home, follow the instructions in the Techniques section on page 136. Trim the canvas edges to 1.5 cm (⅝ in) all around.

2 Measure the exact size of the finished needlepoint. Cut out an oval of thin hard-board or particle board with a coping saw so that it is exactly the same dimensions as the finished needlepoint. Smooth the edges of the wooden oval that will form the base of the coaster by rubbing them evenly with medium-grade sandpaper.

3 Cut approximately a dozen pieces of strong adhesive tape and place them at regular intervals around the perimeter of the canvas. The sticky side of the adhesive tape should be on the wrong side of the finished needlepoint.

4 With a pair of sharp sewing scissors cut notches all around the canvas perimeter; this will prevent additional bulk when the completed coaster lies flat. Place the needlepoint so that it is centred over the wooden oval backing (a). Make sure that no part of the canvas perimeter is folded double on the underside of the coaster as this will make the surface uneven. Trim away more canvas if necessary to reduce bulk. Place strong glue around the perimeter of the underside of the wooden oval. (For the precise quantity of glue that you should apply, follow the manufacturer's instructions.) With your thumb and forefinger, tightly fold the notched edges of the canvas perimeter in toward the middle of the underside of the wooden oval. Firmly press down the pieces of sticky tape so that the needlepoint is stretched tightly around the wooden oval backing (b).

5 Allow the glue to dry according to the manufacturer's instructions. Cut out an oval of the felt backing fabric that measures exactly the same size as dimensions of the wooden oval and glue this to the underside of the coaster (c). The felt backing will conceal the bottom of the coaster and will prevent scratching on a wooden surface. Leave the coaster under a weight, for example several heavy books, overnight; this will help to flatten the edges.

TOMATO PLACEMAT

This project is part of a table setting on a fruit and vegetable theme. I designed it to form a trio with my lemon coaster (see page 118) and my pea napkin ring (see page 126). On a trip to an open-air market in the South of France I was overwhelmed by the quantities of beautiful fruit and vegetables, the tempting smells of breads and cakes and the generally frenetic atmosphere. I had taken my camera with me and I jostled with the shoppers to get a good view of some of the wonderful dispalys of food and to take some photographs in order to use as needlepoint source material. In one corner of the market the local farmers were selling their produce. They had come in from their smallholdings in the hills of Provence with boxfuls of home-grown produce, including plums, baby courgettes or zucchini, onions, dark figs and round, ripe tomatoes.

The tomatoes grabbed my attention instantly and I began painting them and planning a design from the photographs I had taken. By doing this I realized how many shades of red there are in one tomato!

I thought that a tomato placemat would be appetizing and make a decorative addition to any table. In fact the mat would also look attractive under a bowl of fruit or a vase of flowers. Take a look at the photograph opposite and you will see that the placemat is designed so that most of the detail lies around the edges, as I did not want all the interest to be hidden underneath a plate.

I cannot claim to be the first needlepoint designer to have been inspired by vegetables. Whoever deserves that credit, one of the best-known interpreters of vegetables in needlepoint is Kaffe Fassett. His superb depictions of cabbages and cauliflowers, with their spectacular degree of detail, have opened many people's eyes to the wonderfully varied colours, forms and textures to be found in these familiar foods. Keep your own eyes open and you will discover what a wealth of organic subject matter there is close at hand to inspire you. You may just be able to reach out and see what lies in your vegetable rack or fruit bowl for ideas.

To back the placemat I chose a quilted cotton fabric, which is washable and which gives the piece extra body. I selected a dark, rich green for the backing which perfectly complemented the bright red of the tomatoes. A dark shade is practical for use in the kitchen or dining room as it helps to conceal stains. If you cannot find a suitable quilted fabric you can buy a piece of cotton and some lightweight wadding and quilt the cotton by machine or by hand.

opposite: Ripe tomatoes on display in a French market inspired this placemat design. The edges of the placemat, which will not be obscured by a plate, are most detailed. (Caroline Robins)

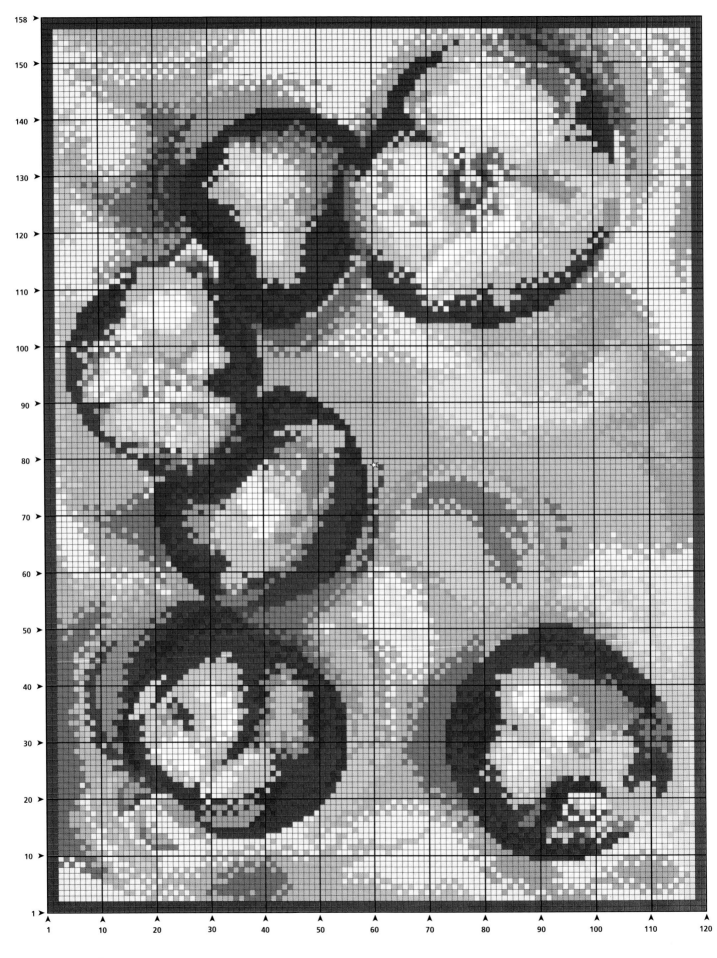

TOMATO PLACEMAT

a

b

c

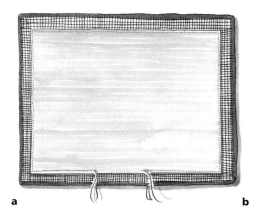

8302 (1)	8880 (1)	8200 (3)	8120 (1)
8236 (1)	8214 (1)	8582 (1)	8156 (1)
9252 (2)	9262 (1)	8322 (1)	9612 (1)
8196 (1)	8134 (1)	8052 (1)	8714 (1)
9100 (1)	8312 (1)	8234 (1)	8874 (1)
9094 (1)	8982 (1)	8294 (1)	8002 (1)
8192 (1)	9614 (1)		

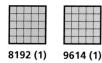

☆ **Mid-point of design**

Use Anchor tapestry wool in the colours and quantities given in the key on the left. The initial numbers refer to the Anchor codes; the numbers that follow in brackets refer to the number of skeins required. A 10 m (11 yd) skein will work approximately 950 stitches. (For DMC equivalents, see the conversion chart on page 141.)

MATERIALS & EQUIPMENT

10-gauge canvas, 40 x 50 cm (16 x 20 in)
Piece of quilted fabric, 34 x 42 cm
(13½ x 17 in) for backing
Sewing thread to match backing fabric
Size 18 tapestry needle

Measures about 30 x 39 cm (12 x 15½ in)
Use one strand of thread for stitching

Making up instructions

1 First block or stretch the finished needlepoint. I strongly recommend that you have this done by a professional. However, if you choose to do it yourself at home, follow the instructions in the Techniques section on page 136. Trim the canvas edges to 2 cm (¾ in) all around.

2 Pin the needlepoint and quilted backing fabric together with right sides facing. Baste, then stitch just inside the edge of the needlepoint in order to prevent any bare canvas from showing. Leave a gap of about 18 cm (7 in) in one side to turn the placemat right side out (a).

3 Trim the seam allowances to 1 cm (⅜ in), cutting across the corners diagonally to reduce bulk (b). Turn the placemat right side out. Press the work from the fabric side, paying special attention to the corners.

4 Slipstitch (c) the opening edges of the gap together neatly (see Techniques, page 138) and press again. In addition, you may find it helpful to put the placemat under a weight, for example some heavy books for a few days; this helps to flatten the edges and provides a smooth surface.

PEA NAPKIN RING

This small-scale project forms part of my fruit and vegetables table setting; it accompanies the lemon coaster (see page 118) and the tomato placemat (see page 123). In order for the napkin ring to harmonize with the colours in the two previous projects, I settled for a predominance of green in the design to match the yellow of the coaster and the warm reds in the placemat.

I began the design process by delving through my reference material and gathered together various photographs, sketches and reproductions of paintings of fruits and vegetables, including peas. First, I made a selection of the most appealing images and pinned these up on my wall to consider them a little longer. I then made some watercolour paintings which were specifically designed to suit the piece of needlepoint. The first stage was to decide on the shape and size of the needlepoint and once I had worked out the dimensions I drew the elongated rectangle, which would be joined at the short ends to circle a napkin, out onto paper and began adding the colour in the form of a pea pod. If you have never tried drawing or painting your own needlepoint designs, then I urge you to do so. You may find it less difficult than you think. I usually work in watercolour, because I love the magical way that the colours merge when the pigment, water and paper make contact. Wonderful, unexpected shapes, sometimes verging on the abstract, can result and the subtle nuances of colour can suggest surprising ideas for choosing yarns. However, watercolour does require a little practice, so you might prefer to use another kind of paint, or perhaps crayons, pastels or felt-tip pens instead. Before you commit your own design to canvas it is a good idea to make a colour palette and experiment with colours and their combinations on paper *before* you go to the expense of buying yarns.

The napkin ring illustrated opposite is worked in silk threads, but you can achieve a similar effect with stranded cotton. Felt is an ideal fabric for backing the work and it is often sold in small squares in department stores and craft shops. I was so pleased with the way that my first pea napkin ring turned out that I decided to repeat the design to see how it would look when enlarged. So, I copied it onto some 8-gauge canvas and used tapestry wool, doubled for extra thickness, for the stitching. I quickly covered the canvas and the design soon grew into an enormous, colourful pea pod. It is fascinating to see just how different a design can look by adjusting the scale.

opposite: A pod full of fresh, green peas seemed the perfect vegetable for a napkin ring. The project is stitched on a fine canvas to allow for added detail. (Caroline Robins)

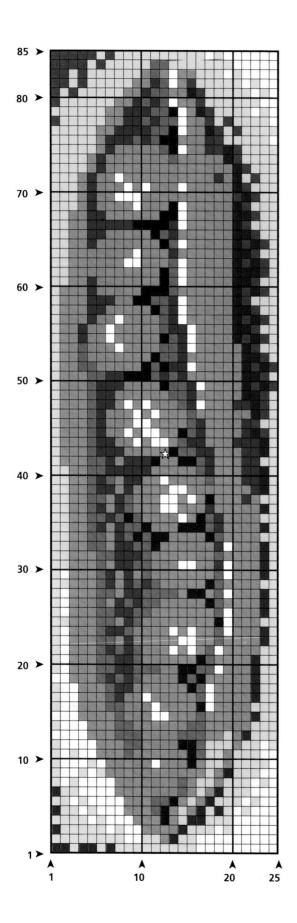

Use Anchor stranded cotton in the colours and quantities given in the key below. The initial numbers refer to the Anchor yarns; the numbers that follow in brackets refer to the number of skeins required. An 8 m (9 yd) skein will work approximately 1,450 stitches. (For DMC equivalents, see the conversion chart on page 140.)

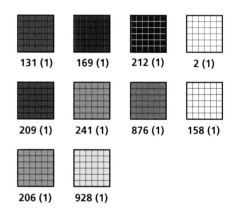

131 (1)   169 (1)   212 (1)   2 (1)

209 (1)   241 (1)   876 (1)   158 (1)

206 (1)   928 (1)

☆ Mid-point of design

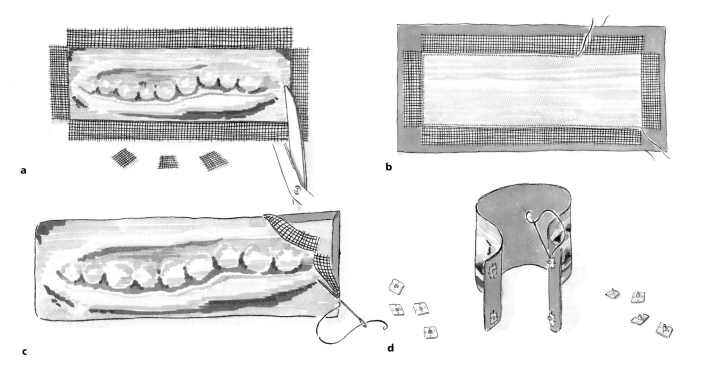

a

b

c

d

MATERIALS & EQUIPMENT

18-gauge canvas, 13 x 22 cm (5 x 9 in)

Piece of felt, 5.5 x 14 cm (2¼ x 5½ in)

Two clear plastic press studs or snaps

Sewing thread to match felt

Size 20 tapestry needle

Measures 3.5 x 12 cm (1½ x 4¾ in)

Use all six strands of thread for stitching

Making up instructions

1 First block or stretch the finished needlepoint. I strongly recommend that you have this done by a professional. However, if you choose to do it yourself at home, follow the instructions in the Techniques section on page 136. Trim the canvas edges to 1 cm (⅜ in) all around. Cut away the excess canvas at the four corners (a) in order to reduce bulk; this is important with such a small item, on which bulky corners would be especially noticeable.

2 Place the finished needlepoint right side down on the felt backing fabric. (You can use an alternative backing, such as a strong cotton, so long as it is of comparable weight to the needlepoint.) Pin and baste the two layers together, then machine stitch, just inside the edge of the needlepoint to prevent any bare canvas from showing. If you do not have access to a sewing machine, you can use backstitch instead (see Techniques, page 137). Begin stitching approximately a quarter of the way along the top right-hand edge of the needlepoint and continue stitching in an anti-clockwise direction, finishing at the lower right-hand corner. This leaves an opening in one corner for turning out (b).

3 Trim the canvas and felt edges close to the line of stitching and cut diagonally across the corners of the felt to reduce bulk. Turn the work right side out. Press with an iron. Do not iron directly on to the needlepoint; protect with a cloth.

4 Fold in the unstitched needlepoint and felt edges in the opening and neatly slip-stitch (c) them together (see page 138). Press the whole piece once again.

5 Sew one half of each press stud or snap to the four corners of the flat napkin ring (d) and press them together to form a ring.

techniques

MATERIALS & EQUIPMENT

CANVAS

When you first take up needlepoint, you may become somewhat confused by the variety of materials available on the market, in particular the different types of canvas, some of which have a variety of names. In our opinion, it doesn't usually matter whether you use a single-thread, double-thread or an interlock canvas, so long as the canvas is of good quality; if you are going to spend several months or longer working on a project then you need to know that it is going to stay in one piece. The colour of the canvas is not especially important either. So long as the threads that form the canvas construction are well covered by the stitches then the colour beneath should not be visible from the right side of the needlepoint. White, beige and yellow are the most widely available colours. The main consideration when choosing canvas is the gauge, or the number of threads or holes over 1 in (2.5 cm). Canvas gauges range from the fantastically fine 32-gauge, which we suggest you avoid if you value your sanity and eyesight, right through to 4- or even 3-gauge, which are ideal for wall hangings or rugs, but which eat up huge amounts of yarn. For the projects in this book we have specified which gauge to use in each case, but you can alter the gauge if you wish to increase or decrease the size of the finished piece. The type of canvas that you use is your personal choice. However, some are more suitable than others for particular purposes.

Double-thread canvas, which is also called Penelope canvas, is very flat and smooth and is perfect for small projects such as buttons or tie pins. It is easy to work on and keeps its shape well. If you wish, you can work different sizes of stitches together, using smaller stitches over one thread and larger ones over both threads. This is a soft canvas and it doesn't require stiffening to hold its shape as the weave itself does that for you. The gauge of double-thread canvas is given as the number of holes per 1 in (2.5 cm). The number of threads is twice the number of holes.

Single-thread or mono canvas comes in a larger range of sizes and is available in several colours. It is easy to use and highly recommended, especially for those with poor eyesight. It is a strong canvas and is used in many kits. However, it does fray easily which can pose problems in the making up stage. To prevent fraying you can bind the edges with masking tape. The threads are easier to see on single-thread canvas than they are on double-thread canvas.

Interlock canvas is a recent development. It looks like single-thread canvas, but the vertical threads are actually pairs of threads which are twisted around the horizontal threads. This gives the canvas great stability, so that distortion is minimal.

Choosing the canvas appropriate to your way of working is, to some extent, a matter of trial and error. We suggest that you try out the different types and see which kind you prefer. When buying or cutting out canvas for a project, you should allow a margin of 5 cm (2 in) or more around the stitched area. Before you begin to stitch, bind the edges with masking tape to prevent fraying; this also prevents the stitching threads from snagging on the canvas edges as you work your needle.

THREADS

Threads come in a range of weights and thicknesses. Ideally the thread you select should conceal the canvas completely. There are various types of threads available, with different characteristics.

Tapestry wool is a 4-ply yarn and is a perfect complement for 10-, 12- and 14-gauge canvas. Used double thickness it also works well on 7- or 8-gauge canvas. Needlepoint worked in wool has a matte finish.

Stranded cotton has been used for many of the projects in this book. This is ideal for working on finer canvas, such as 16- and 18-gauge; all six strands of the thread are used. The colours are generally vibrant and come in an enormous range. The finished texture of needlepoint worked in stranded cotton has a jewel-like sheen that catches the light.

Soft or matte embroidery cotton is a sort of halfway house between wool and stranded cotton. The colours have the same rich intensity of stranded cotton, but the yarn is thicker and the texture of the needlepoint is matte. Soft cotton works well on 12- or 14-mesh canvas.

Other threads that are widely used for needlepoint (although not for any of the projects featured in this book) are crewel and Persian wool. Crewel is a fine yarn which can be used in any number of strands, so it is particularly versatile. Persian wool is a triple-strand yarn and the strands (which are thicker than crewel) tend to separate easily.

NEEDLES

For working needlepoint always use a tapestry needle. This has a blunt point, which does not split the threads or catch on the canvas, and a large eye for easy threading. Tapestry needles come in various sizes, from 13 (the largest) to 26 (the smallest). For making up the projects you will need sharp-pointed needles such as sharps, betweens or crewels.

SEWING MACHINE

This is a useful – but not an essential – piece of equipment for making up the projects. If you haven't got a sewing machine you can use backstitch (see page 137) wherever the instructions call for machine stitching.

SCISSORS

You will need two pairs: a large pair of dressmaker's shears for cutting canvas and other fabrics and small, sharp-pointed embroidery scissors for cutting threads.

IRON

A steam iron is extremely useful in the making-up process. You can substitute this with a dry iron and a damp pressing cloth. Never use an iron directly on your needlepoint as it may damage the stitching; always protect it with a cloth.

SEWING THREAD

When making up a needlepoint item, it is important to use thread that will not break easily when it is pulled through thick materials and subjected to strain. A cotton-covered polyester thread is ideal; the polyester core gives strength, while the cotton exterior will withstand a hot iron. You can now buy a pure polyester thread that is intended for use on all fabrics and will tolerate a hot iron. However, make sure that any polyester thread you use is clearly marked as suitable for all fabrics.

OTHER USEFUL EQUIPMENT

The following items will be useful on occasion:

Masking tape, use this to bind the canvas edges so as to prevent fraying.

Fabric marking pen, or tailor's chalk, use for marking design outlines onto canvas. Always use a waterproof needlepoint pen and *never* an ordinary felt-tip pen which is likely to run and may ruin your work.

A blunt knitting needle or a pair of tweezers, use for pushing out corners when turning a piece of stitched work right side out.

Compass, set square or right-angled triangle and ruler for accurate measuring.

Calculator for accurate calculations.

TECHNIQUES

NEEDLEPOINT STITCHES

Although there are many needlepoint stitches which give interesting textural effects, we have used only the simplest stitch for the projects in the book: tent stitch. One reason for this is that we want anyone to be able to learn the basics of the craft quickly and start enjoying it straightaway. Another reason is the smooth finish of tent stitch enables us to concentrate on colours and shapes rather than textures, and because it is the smallest of all needlepoint stitches it is most suitable for depicting detail and curved lines.

CONTINENTAL TENT STITCH

There are two different ways to produce tent stitch. (There is also a similar stitch, half-cross, which we do not recommend as it does not cover the canvas well.) We recommend the form called "continental" which is worked in horizontal or vertical rows. To learn this simple stitch, practise it on a small piece of 14-gauge single-thread canvas, about 15 cm (6 in) square, using a size 18 tapestry needle threaded with one strand of tapestry wool. For this sample cut the strand about 30 cm (12 in) long. For the projects, use a thread no longer than 45 cm (18 in) to prevent fraying.

1 To secure the thread temporarily, make a knot in one end and insert the needle from front to back, about 3 cm (1 in) to the left of your chosen starting point. This thread end will be covered by the stitching. Do not begin with a knot on the wrong side, as this is likely to pull through to the front.

2 Bring the needle up at the starting point A and take it down one thread up and one to the right B. This completes one stitch. (See above right.)

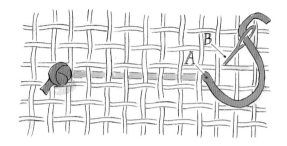

3 Bring the needle up at C, which is one thread to the left of A and take it down at D, which is one to the left of B. (See below.)

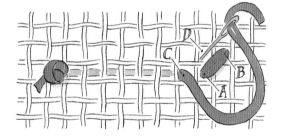

Continue working the needle and yarn in the same way, working in the same direction – from right to left. When you have nearly reached the knot, cut it off, then continue as before. (See below.)

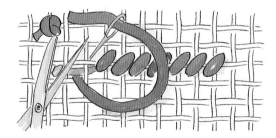

Now work another row of stitches, in the opposite direction – from left to right, one row above the first row. Bring the needle up at E, take it down at F then up at G and down at H. Continue along the row in the same way. (See above right.)

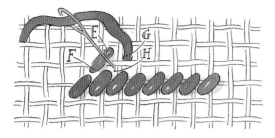

Note that it is always preferable to bring the needle up in an empty hole rather than in one containing a stitch. This produces a neater, smoother effect. Bringing the needle up in a partially full hole tends to split the threads and blur the outline of the stitches.

In order to fasten a thread end, you simply run the needle through four or five stitches on the wrong side of the needlepoint and cut it off. Then start a new thread by running it through existing work on the wrong side or by fastening it temporarily with a knot, as already described.

If you turn the sample over, you will see that on the wrong side the stitches are longer than on the right side. This gives a smooth effect and creates a firm, hardwearing fabric. (See below.)

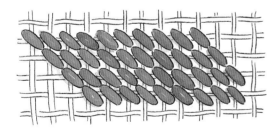

However, this method of stitching does tend to distort the canvas threads somewhat. You can minimize the distortion by working in a frame – although we don't use one, as it makes the work less portable and rather less enjoyable as it eliminates most of the tactile aspect of the work. Or you can adjust your stitching tension (see stitching techniques) to reduce

the strain on the canvas threads. Interlock canvas will also prevent much distortion. Another alternative is to use the basketweave form of tent stitch.

BASKETWEAVE TENT STITCH

This alternative form of tent stitch is worked in diagonal rows and gets its name from the woven effect produced on the wrong side of the needlepoint. It is especially good for large areas of colour and distorts the canvas very little. However, it can be rather fiddly to position in small areas. Begin the stitch in the upper right-hand corner or row of the area and work downward and outward. (See below.)

STITCHING TECHNIQUES

To make your needlepoint enjoyable, here are some suggestions that you may find useful. First, try to work with a smooth, moderate tension. If you pull the stitches too tightly the canvas will become distorted and the thread will be stretched and appear thin. If your tension is too loose, you will end up with loops on the front of the canvas. Ideally the tension should be smooth and even across the whole piece.

We recommend you work without a frame. There are two ways of forming the stitches. Either "stab" the needle up and down, which requires two movements for each stitch (use this method if working on a frame). Or "sew" the stitches by taking the needle under the mesh in one movement, then draw the thread through, so always keeping the hand on the right side of the work. To help achieve an even tension, work from the middle of the design outward. Don't, for example, fill in isolated areas of colour and then try to fill in the gaps; work evenly outward to the edges of the piece. Unpicking needlepoint is not fun and can be disheartening if you discover you have been stitching in the wrong direction for hours!

If you do need to unpick an area, take great care in doing so. Using a small pair of sharp-pointed embroidery scissors snip through each stitch individually and then, using a needle or a pair of tweezers, carefully remove the loose, cut threads. It is not a major disaster if you accidentally cut through the canvas mesh. Simply cut out a small patch of the same size canvas and baste it to the back of the damaged area, making sure that the threads of the two meshes align exactly. The new stitching will cover the joins and make for an invisible mend.

BLOCKING OR STRETCHING

It is essential to block your needlepoint when it is completed. This process, which is also called stretching, transforms the finished needlepoint from a misshapen, crumpled bundle into work of art! Instructions for blocking are given below. However, we strongly recommend that you get this done by a professional, if possible. They have the most up-to-date equipment which will produce superior results. Ask your local needlepoint shop if they provide this service or can recommend someone who does.

To block your needlepoint yourself, you will need:

A large piece of hardboard or particleboard

A piece of white paper

Masking tape

A ruler and set square

Nails and a hammer

Cloth for dampening, or a plastic spray bottle

Wallpaper paste, container and paintbrush

1 Tape the piece of paper to the hardboard. Using a waterproof pen and the set square, draw a right angle on the paper, which should be visible through the canvas mesh. (See below.)

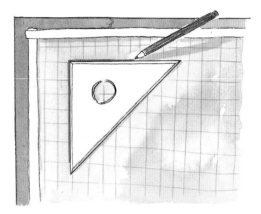

2 Place the needlepoint face down on the board with the top left-hand corner of the work just inside the drawn right angle; this applies only to a needlepoint that is rectangular in shape. If it is an odd shape you need to draw the outline of the whole design on the paper. This may involve tracing the original design and positioning the tracing over the white paper.

3 Hammer a nail into the canvas at this corner, about 3 cm (1 in) outside the stitched area. (See below.)

4 Now pull your canvas down at the corner. Put a nail into the spare canvas at this edge. Check with the set square that the needlepoint forms a right angle and adjust it if necessary. Pull tightly at the top right-hand corner and nail this down in the same way. Repeat this at the bottom left-hand corner. Again, check the corners with the set square. (See below.)

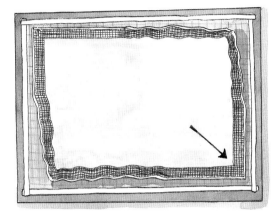

5 When all the corners of the needlepoint have been nailed in place, stretch and nail securely midway along the sides of the canvas edges. All the time you should be pulling the needlepoint gently in order to make it absolutely square. Check with the set square and ruler that the sides are even and that all the corners are square. Continue to stretch and nail until you are completely satisfied that the work is the correct shape. (See below.)

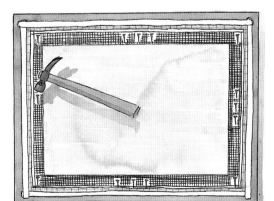

6 Dab the back of the canvas with a damp cloth, or spray it evenly with water from a spray bottle.

7 Make up a small amount of wallpaper paste, following the manufacturer's instructions, in a container such as an old tin or a jar. Using the paintbrush, dab the paste evenly and not too thickly onto the back of the needlepoint – this will help to hold the threads in place. The fungicide present in the paste will also protect the work from mould if it is kept in damp surroundings. (See below.)

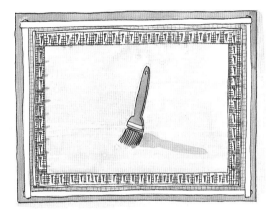

8 Leave the work for a minimum of two days for the best results. Make sure that it is thoroughly dry, then remove the nails. Leave the edges (including the masking tape) untrimmed until you are ready to make up the item.

STITCHES USED IN MAKING UP

BACKSTITCH

This stitch can be used as an alternative to machine stitching. Take in only two needlepoint stitches or canvas threads with each stitch. (See below.)

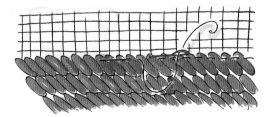

OVERSEWING OR OVERCASTING

This stitch can be used to neaten a raw edge or to join two edges. In the second case the stitches are kept very small and worked close together. (See below.)

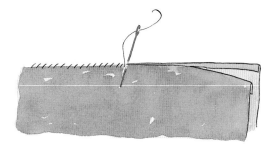

SLIPSTITCH

This stitch is often used to join two turned-under edges almost invisibly, or to hem a turned-in edge in place. Keep the stitches small and neat and work in a continuous movement. (See below.)

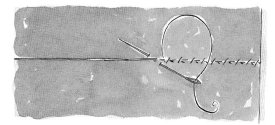

BASTING

This is simply a large running stitch which is used to join two or more layers temporarily in position. Remove basting stitches when the permanent stitching has been completed. (See below.)

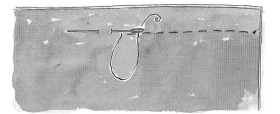

TOPSTITCH

Topstitching holds fabric and canvas layers in place or lends a decorative accent. It is normally worked by machine. You can also use backstitch. (See page 137.)

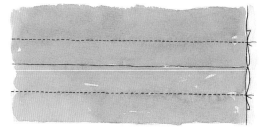

BIAS STRIPS

Strips of fabric cut on the bias are used to bind raw edges decoratively. Cut at a 45° angle to the grain.

1 To mark the first strip, fold the selvedge up to meet the crosswise edge of the fabric (having made sure that it is straight). Pin the edges together, then press along the diagonal fold. (See below.)

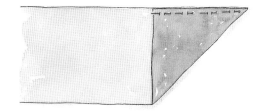

2 Cut along this fold and mark a line parallel to the edge and the specified measurement from it. Mark more strips as required. (See below.)

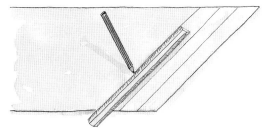

3 To join strips, place them together so that the seam follows the grain of the fabric. Stitch and press the seam open. (See below.)

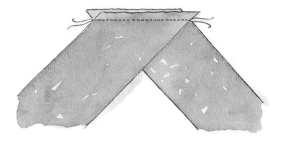

To calculate how much fabric you will need to cut a single bias strip of a given length you should divide the required length by 1.414. For example, to obtain a strip 50 cm (20 in) long, you will need 36 cm (15 in) of fabric. (These figures are rounded up.) Conversely, to find the maximum length of a bias strip cut from a given length of fabric, you can multiply the fabric length by 1.414.

TRANSFERRING A DESIGN ONTO CANVAS

Throughout this book we hope we have encouraged you to have a go at creating your own original designs. This is much less complicated than you may think and all you need is the inspiration, the confidence and the basic materials – yarns, canvas and a few simple drawing materials.

Designs can grow out of the smallest doodles and their scale can change radically, depending on what you decide to make with the final piece. To start, draw the finished shape and fill in the design. Tracing paper can be indispensable at this stage, see the Alphabet picture project on page 46. Then you can decide on the size of the finished piece. Either you can visit a photocopy shop and enlarge or reduce your design mechanically, or else you can scale it up or down by hand, see scaling up a design.

SCALING UP A DESIGN

1 Draw a grid over the design, or onto a piece of tracing paper laid over it. Designs given in needlepoint books or magazines will already have a grid.

2 On a larger sheet of paper, draw another grid containing exactly the same number of lines but spaced farther apart, so that the squares are larger than those on the original grid by the required amount. For example, if the design needs to be twice the size of the original you should make the squares twice as large. (See below.)

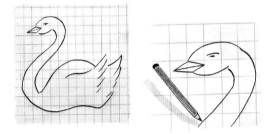

3 Copy the design outlines onto the new grid, positioning them as on the original grid. In the same way, the same method, using smaller squares for the new grid, can be used to reduce a design.

MEASUREMENT CONVERSIONS

In this book metric measurements are given first, followed by imperial equivalents. The equivalents are often approximate and may vary from one context to another. This is to avoid giving a measurement in either system that is unnecessarily precise and awkward to handle. For example, the nearest equivalent of 30 cm is 11⅞ in; but the equivalent normally given is 12 in. This approach also allows small measurements within each system to add up correctly. The golden rule to follow is to work in one system *or* the other. Choose one system of measurement and stick to it!

139

CONVERSION CHART

This conversion chart gives DMC equivalents of Anchor stranded cottons and soft matte embroidery cottons. Use it only as a guide as it is not always possible to provide exact comparisons. Anchor shades in brackets indicate the nearest equivalent shade. An * indicates that the Anchor shade has been used more than once and care should be taken to avoid duplication within a design.

DMC	Anchor	DMC	Anchor	DMC	Anchor	DMC	Anchor	DMC	Anchor	DMC	Anchor	DMC	Anchor
BLANC	1	414	235	608	333	772	259	893	27	964	185	3364	260
ECRU	387	415	398	610	889	775	128	894	26	966	240	3371	382
208	111	420	374	611	898	776	24	895	269*	970	324*	3607	87
209	109	422	943	612	832	778	968*	898	359	971	316*	3608	86
210	108	433	371	613	853	780	310	899	(40)	972	298	3609	85
211	342	434	365	632	936	781	309*	900	(326*)	973	290	3685	69
221	897	435	901*	640	393*	782	308	902	72	975	370	3687	68
223	895*	436	363	642	392	783	307	904	258	976	(309*)	3688	66
224	893	437	362	644	391	791	178	905	257	977	313	3689	49
225	892	444	291	645	273*	792	177	906	256	986	246	3705	35
300	352	445	288	646	8581*	793	176	907	255	987	244	3706	33
301	349*	451	233	647	8581*	794	175	909	923	988	243	3708	31
304	47	452	232	648	900*	796	133	910	230*	989	242	3712	10*
307	289	453	231	666	46	797	132	911	230*	991	(189)	3713	968*
309	42	469	267*	676	891	798	131	912	205	992	187*	3716	25
310	403	470	266*	677	300*	799	145	913	204	993	186*	3721	896*
311	148	471	265	680	901*	800	144	915	972	995	410	3722	895*
312	979	472	(278)	699	229	801	358	917	89	996	433	3726	970
315	(896*)	498	(43)	700	228	806	169*	918	341*	3011	845	3727	969*
316	969*	500	879	701	227	807	168*	919	340	3012	843	3731	(38)
317	400	501	878	702	226	809	130	920	339	3013	842	3733	75*
318	399	502	877	703	239	813	160	921	338	3021	905*	3740	872
319	(217)	503	876	704	238	814	45	922	337	3022	(899*)	3743	869
320	215	504	875	712	926	815	22	924	851	3023	(899*)	3746	118*
321	9046	517	170	718	88	816	(44)	926	850	3024	900*	3747	120
322	978	518	(168*)	720	326*	817	19	927	848	3031	360*	3750	(123)
326	59	519	(167*)	721	324*	818	48	928	847	3032	903*	3752	976
327	100	520	862*	722	323	819	271	930	922	3033	830	3753	975
333	119	522	860	725	306	820	134	931	921	3041	871	3755	140
334	977	523	859*	726	295	822	390	932	343	3042	870	3756	158*
335	(41)	524	858*	727	293	823	150	934	862*	3045	888	3760	161*
336	149	535	(273*)	729	890	824	164	935	269*	3046	887	3761	9159*
340	118*	543	933	730	924*	825	162	936	846	3047	886	3765	169*
341	117	550	101	731	281*	826	161*	937	268*	3051	861	3766	167*
347	13*	552	99	732	281*	827	9159*	938	381	3052	859*	3768	779
349	13*	553	98	733	280*	828	158*	939	152	3053	858*	3770	276
350	(11)	554	97	734	279	829	906	943	188	3064	883	3772	914*
351	10*	561	212	738	361	830	277*	945	881	3072	274	3773	882
352	9*	562	210	739	366	831	277*	946	332	3078	292	3774	778*
353	6	563	208	740	316*	832	907*	947	330	3325	129	3776	349*
355	341*	564	206*	741	314	833	(907*)	948	778*	3326	36	3777	20
356	5975	580	924*	742	303	834	874	950	4146*	3328	10*	3778	9575
367	(216)	581	280*	743	305	838	380	951	880	3340	329	3779	868*
368	214	597	168*	744	301	839	360*	954	203	3341	328	3781	905*
369	(213)	598	167*	745	300*	840	379	955	206*	3345	268*	3782	831
370	856	600	78	746	386	841	378	956	54	3346	267*	3787	(393*)
371	855	601	77	747	928	842	376	957	52	3347	266*	3790	903*
372	854	602	63	754	4146*	844	273*	958	187*	3348	264	3799	236
400	351	603	62	758	868*	869	944	959	186*	3350	65		
402	347	604	55	760	9*	890	(683)	961	76	3354	74		
407	914*	605	50	761	23	891	29	962	75*	3362	263		
413	401	606	335	762	234	892	28	963	73	3363	262		

The Anchor shades listed below do not appear on this conversion chart, as they are unique to the Anchor range.

2	92	112	142	218	275	355	375	844	920
8	94	121	143	225	297	357	388	849	939
39	95	122	146	241	302	367	397	852	940
57	96	127	147	245	304	368	681	873	941
60	102	136	159	253	311	369		884	942
70	103	137	209	254	334	372		885	945
90	110	139	211	261	336	373		894	956

This conversion chart gives DMC equivalents of Anchor tapestry wools. It should only be used as a guide since it is not always possible to provide exact comparisons.

DMC	Anchor	DMC	Anchor	DMC	Anchor	DMC	Anchor	DMC	Anchor	DMC	Anchor	DMC	Anchor
7078	8014	7196	8368	7285	9790	7361	9212	7437	8156	7513	9388	7626	9792
7102	8256	7198	8242	7287	8834	7362	9214	7439	8164	7514	9392	7632	9600
7103	8434	7199	8404	7288	8838	7363	9216	7444	9526	7515	9662	7640	8440
7104	8212	7200	9612	7289	8840	7364	9202	7445	9536	7518	9368	7650	8822
7105	8396	7202	8412	7292	8714	7367	9204	7446	9560	7519	9366	7666	8202
7106	8214	7204	8414	7293	8718	7369	9014	7447	8264	7420	9654	7676	9288
7107	8204	7205	8418	7294	8836	7370	9004	7448	9602	7521	9364	7677	9286
7108	8218	7207	8402	7295	8738	7371	9302	7449	8354	7523	9324	7678	9284
7110	8220	7208	8424	7296	8824	7372	9684	7450	9362	7524	9404	7679	9282
7115	8354	7209	8352	7297	8838	7373	9258	7451	9632	7525	9388	7680	8094
7119	8428	7210	8420	7298	8814	7375	8514	7452	9442	7526	9662	7681	8092
7120	9614	7211	8482	7299	8742	7376	9176	7453	9442	7527	9372	7690	8900
7121	8342	7212	8422	7300	9772	7377	9264	7455	8060	7529	9664	7692	8894
7122	8252	7213	8504	7301	8814	7379	9208	7457	9526	7533	9648	7695	8738
7123	8324	7214	8232	7302	8626	7382	9094	7458	9566	7535	9666	7700	9540
7124	8258	7215	8326	7303	8236	7384	9096	7459	9542	7538	9666	7701	8882
7125	8238	7217	8350	7304	8790	7385	9008	7460	9632	7540	8992	7702	8880
7127	8240	7218	8426	7306	8792	7386	9006	7461	9484	7541	9020	7703	8876
7132	8362	7219	8426	7307	8744	7387	9024	7462	9486	7542	9002	7704	9072
7133	8482	7221	8502	7308	8638	7389	9026	7463	9488	7543	9594	7705	8720
7135	8436	7223	8506	7309	9800	7390	9054	7465	9638	7544	8218	7708	8592
7136	8438	7224	9618	7311	8674	7391	9314	7466	9640	7545	8966	7709	8590
7137	8442	7226	8508	7313	8776	7392	9066	7467	9642	7547	9166	7711	8588
7138	8442	7228	8512	7314	8672	7393	9264	7468	9396	7548	9164	7713	9796
7139	8424	7230	9634	7316	8688	7394	9068	7469	9648	7549	9162	7715	8712
7141	9362	7232	9676	7317	8690	7396	9180	7470	8016	7555	8738	7722	9672
7143	9422	7234	9678	7318	8632	7398	9182	7471	8112	7558	9786	7724	9324
7144	9508	7236	9680	7319	8634	7399	8932	7472	8056	7568	8712	7725	8096
7146	8328	7238	9682	7320	9006	7400	9252	7473	8022	7573	9288	7726	8018
7147	8402	7241	8586	7321	8892	7401	9540	7474	8024	7579	8052	7727	8016
7148	9508	7242	8594	7322	8874	7402	9074	7477	9408	7582	9308	7739	8054
7151	8484	7243	8590	7323	8876	7404	9076	7479	9452	7583	9198	7740	8156
7153	8488	7244	8602	7326	8880	7406	9078	7484	8020	7584	9274	7741	8124
7155	8490	7245	8596	7327	8882	7408	9028	7485	8024	7587	8812	7742	8120
7157	8492	7247	8612	7329	8884	7411	9482	7487	8048	7590	8840	7745	8012
7162	9484	7250	9672	7331	9064	7413	9366	7488	9410	7591	8824	7746	8034
7164	8322	7251	8482	7333	8874	7415	9368	7489	9644	7592	8738	7758	8400
7165	8328	7253	8524	7335	8878	7416	9370	7490	9292	7593	8818	7759	8368
7166	9510	7254	8542	7336	8636	7417	9268	7491	9382	7594	8832	7760	8396
7167	8330	7255	8526	7337	8880	7419	9664	7492	9322	7595	8822	7761	8346
7168	8262	7257	8528	7339	8904	7420	9302	7493	9324	7596	8922	7762	8254
7169	8264	7259	8530	7340	9152	7421	9406	7494	9404	7597	8916	7766	8064
7170	9632	7260	8542	7341	9154	7422	9256	7496	9408	7598	8934	7767	8062
7171	9504	7262	8544	7342	9156	7423	9404	7497	8106	7599	8912	7768	9156
7173	9552	7264	8546	7344	9100	7424	9258	7499	9430	7600	8458	7769	9100
7174	9446	7266	8548	7345	9102	7425	9220	7500	9632	7602	8456	7770	9164
7175	9554	7268	8550	7346	9104	7426	9260	7501	9322	7603	8456	7771	9162
7176	9558	7270	9772	7347	9024	7427	9178	7503	8054	7604	8962	7772	9094
7178	9562	7271	9632	7348	9008	7428	9024	7504	8040	7605	8452	7773	9152
7179	8296	7272	9676	7351	9192	7429	9028	7505	8100	7606	8198	7780	8102
7184	8240	7273	9776	7353	9286	7431	8092	7506	8060	7617	9774	7781	8104
7191	9612	7275	9764	7354	8368	7432	9624	7508	8062	7618	9790	7782	8100
7192	8342	7280	9672	7355	9310	7433	8094	7509	9654	7619	9268	7783	8024
7193	8344	7282	9786	7356	8260	7434	8116	7510	9052	7620	9792	7784	8098
7194	8346	7283	8626	7359	9266	7435	8096	7511	9326	7622	9764	7785	8096
7195	8348	7284	8714	7360	8162	7436	8122	7512	9328	7624	9768	7786	8116
7790	8542	7813	8806	7852	8256	7906	8974	7925	8840	7951	8256	7999	8906
7791	8694	7820	8692	7853	8252	7909	8970	7926	8902	7952	8964	BLANC	8000
7796	8692	7823	8694	7860	8924	7911	8988	7927	8898	7954	8984	ECRU	8006
7797	8690	7828	8802	7861	8920	7912	8986	7928	8892	7956	8966	NOIR	9800
7798	8644	7833	9406	7870	9058	7914	8970	7930	8824	7958	8962		
7799	8684	7840	9622	7873	9232	7915	9118	7938	9642	7961	8400		
7800	8682	7845	8064	7875	8234	7917	9552	7943	8972	7971	8120		
7801	9646	7846	8062	7890	9206	7918	9524	7946	8194	7973	8118		
7802	8788	7849	8216	7895	8590	7919	9534	7947	8166	7988	9168		
7804	8454	7850	8212	7896	8524	7920	8236	7949	9620	7995	8808		
7807	8806	7851	8258	7905	8052	7922	9536	7950	9596	7996	8806		

The following companies supply a wide range of yarns. Contact the head offices listed below for further information on local stockists.

In the UK:

Appletons
Thames Works
Church Street
Chiswick
London W4 2PE

Coats Patons Crafts
McMullen Road
Darlington
Co Durham DL1 1YQ
(Anchor yarns.)

DMC Creative World Ltd
Pullman Road
Wigston
Leicestershire LE182DY

The Craft Collection Ltd
Terry Mills
Westfield Road
Horbury
Wakefield
West Yorks WF4 6HD
(Paterna yarns. Also distribute throughout Europe.)

In the US:

Appletons
Distributed by Potpourri Etc
PO Box 78
Redondo Beach
California 90277

Coats and Clark
Greenville
South Carolina
(Anchor yarns.)

The DMC Corporation
Port Kearny
Building 10
South Kearny
New Jersey 07032

JCA Inc
35 Scales Lane
Townshend
Massachusetts 01469
(Head office distributing Patanayan yarns.)

In Australia and New Zealand:

Appletons
Distributed by
Clifton H. Joseph
391-393 Little Lonsdale St
Melbourne
Victoria 3000
Australia

Altamira
34 Murphy Street
South Yarra
Melbourne 3141
Australia
(Head office and distributors of Paterna and Appleton yarns.)

DMC Needlecraft Pty Ltd
51-66 Carrington Road
Marrickville
NSW 2204
Australia
(Head office for Australia and New Zealand.)

Coats Patons Crafts
Mulgrave 3170
Australia
(Anchor yarns.)

Appletons
Distributed by Nancy's
Embroidery Ltd
326 Tinakori Road
Thorndon
Wellington
New Zealand

The Stitching Co Ltd
PO Box 74/269
Market Rd
Auckland
New Zealand
(Head office distributing Paterna yarns.)

In Europe:

Appletons
Distributed by Passe
Recompose
10 rue des Prebends
64100 Bayonne
France
and Appleton's yarns also
distributed by
Kell's Corner
28 rue Vital
75016 Paris
France

Coats Sartel Loisirs
59392 Wattrelos Cedex
France
(Anchor yarns.)

Dollfuss Mieg & Co
10 avenue Ledru-Rollin
75579 Paris
France
(DMC yarns.)

Appletons
Distributed by A Beller
Hoher Weg 28
46446 Emmerich
Germany

Coats Mez GmbH
79337 Kensingen
Germany
(Anchor yarns.)

BTW
Stader landstr. 41-43
D-2820 Bremen 77
Germany
(DMC yarns.)

Cucirini Cantoni Coats
20124 Milano
Italy
(Anchor yarns.)

DMC
Ciale Italia 84
1-20020 Lainate
Milano
Italy

DMC
7/9 rue du Pavillon
B-1210 Brussels
Belgium
(Head office for Benelux countries.)

The following addresses are useful for completing the projects featured in the book:

The Costume Jewellery
Component Co
95 Crown Road
East Twickenham
Middlesex TW1 3EX
(Supplies button, tie pin and brooch kits, see the project on page 104.)

Creativity Yarns
35-37 New Oxford Street
London WC1
(This shop stocks a large range of yarns and canvases; they also offer a professional blocking or stretching service.)

Gilbey's Waistcoat Gallery
2 New Burlington Place
Savile Row
London W1
(Provides a waistcoat making-up service, see the Bloomsbury waistcoat project on page 68.)

The Bead Shop
43 Neal Street
Covent Garden
London WC2
(This shop supplies a wide range of decorative beads, see the spectacles case project on page 108.)

ACKNOWLEDGEMENTS

above: needlepoint designed for a mirror case by Caroline Robins

My thanks to family and friends who gave me so much support and to
Paul at Creativity Yarns for his invaluable assistance.

Caroline Robins

Many thanks to Paul Beeson at Creativity Yarns for all his help, advice and enthusiasm,
see the Directory on page 142.
Thanks also to all my chums for their support and interest in the projects, especially Margaret
Horrocks, Jean Braid, Andy Grogan, Mike McGee and Angela Tambini and Mina Martinez. A big
thank you to Rosalind Dallas who started off the chain of events that led to the book happening.
And special thanks to my mum who launched me into sewing at such an early age and to my
grandmother whose glorious cushion provided me with so much inspiration.

Christine Büttner

The publishers would also like to thank Jan Barnes and Mrs Elvin of the Royal School of
Needlework, Mr and Mrs Owen and The Bead Shop, see the Directory on page 142.